The Cook Survives . . . is the ideal series of cookbooks for special occasions and particular situations. Designed by Pat McCormack to help you – the cook – enjoy yourself and keep on top of things in the kitchen, *The Cook Survives* . . . series offers useful hints for organizing your cooking, easy-to-cook tasty menus and detailed recipes packed with helpful information.

The Cook Survives . . . *Children's Parties* is the ideal companion when you are preparing that special treat for the kids.

By the same author

The Cook Survives . . . Christmas and New Year
The Cook Survives . . . Bedsitland

PAT McCORMACK

The Cook Survives . . .
Children's Parties

Illustrated by Geraldine Foster

GRAFTON BOOKS
A Division of the Collins Publishing Group

LONDON GLASGOW
TORONTO SYDNEY AUCKLAND

Grafton Books
A Division of the Collins Publishing Group
8 Grafton Street, London W1X 3LA

Published by Grafton Books 1986

ISBN 0-586-06640-3

Printed and bound in Great Britain by
Collins, Glasgow

Set in Bembo

Contents

Acknowledgements

Special thanks for their help in compiling this book must go to:

Nicola and Jason Penney
Tara and Rosine Derricott
Faye Brown
Janet Harris
John McCormack
Ryan Skidmore
Mark Sherratt

Introduction

Introduction

Arranging a party for youngsters can prove rather daunting; it will be announced that Sean-at-school had a clown and magician to his party, while Jodie took about twenty friends to a very expensive theme park – and then the next thing to contend with is the current trend of American soap operas of turning the back garden into Disneyland at the very least! Oh, dear!

The Cook Survives . . . will hopefully solve your problems by combining a practical and down-to-earth approach with just a little bit of fantasy! Imaginative presentation always makes such a difference and is especially effective when the basic idea is carried on throughout the party. The following pages have lots of easy-to-do ideas that will transform any table-setting, room or garden.

One of the trickier aspects of organizing a children's party is to choose dishes that are popular with kids, interesting to make, and special enough for a party. *The Cook Survives . . . Children's Parties* has recipes that have been especially chosen to make short work of such problems!

The activities chosen for your guests will be very important. Our younger 'panel of advisors' (4–7 years old) put 'games' at the top of their lists of 'most favourite things about parties'. The older advisors (8–14 years old) put disco or video parties in the number one slot with the boys at least being more than willing to sit through a full-length film (providing it was one of their own choosing!). There is a chapter later in the book which lists all our advisors' most favourite games, with instructions on how-to-play the more obscure ones.

Each particular party is treated individually, and with ideas for food, decor and, of course, a special cake collected together in the relevant chapter it becomes remarkably easy and hassle-free to make a resounding success of children's parties!

The Parties

1 Afternoon tea-party for 1–2 year olds

The very thought of having a party for crawlers and
toddlers can be a bit off-putting but, incongruous as it
may seem, a formal tea-party spread works well for 1–2
year olds, the small dainty sandwiches and cakes being
particularly suitable for tiny fingers.

2 Teddy-bear's Picnic for 2–5 year olds

A good party for toddlers that is really enjoyable when
held outside, but easy enough to move indoors if the
weather is unkind. A large, checked tablecloth and the
liberal use of a quick free-hand teddy-bear shape are
the only essential items!

3 'Our Most Favourite Things' Party for 4–6 year olds

Take all the number one choices of party food from our
young advisors, combine with their most popular games
and the result will inevitably be a success – but even with
a party format as well-tried and tested as this, having a
surprise or two up your sleeve will keep the excitement
going and give just the right edge.

4   Cowboy Party for 4–6 year olds

Super heroes come and go but cowboys are forever! This is the easiest party to do. 'Fancy dress' along with beans and sausages as essential items in your 'chuck-wagon' spread, will provide a party that few little 'cowboys' (or 'cowgirls' for that matter) could resist!

5   Fairy Princess Party for 4–7 year olds

The party for a little girl (sorry boys!). With lots and lots of silver everywhere, silver flowers, silver bells and silver ribbons, dolls dressed in white with silver tinsel in their hair, spun-sugar webs twinkling around little cakes and the prettiest fantasy cake you ever saw, all go to make this the most beautiful of parties. (Sounds complicated? Not if you raid the Christmas-tree decorations box!)

6   Christmas Party for 4–7 year olds

Having Father Christmas in attendance makes a lovely feature for this most seasonal of parties. Decor is easy, since it probably will have already been done for the festive season and won't need dismantling immediately after the party!

There is no reason why this shouldn't be suitable as a birthday party too; the reindeer-and-sleigh cake looks super with candles.

7 Bar-b-que Party for 6+ year olds

There is nothing like the smell of a bar-b-que or the sight of children actually queuing happily for food, clutching their plates and waiting for 'more' – it is a scene that owes nothing to *Oliver Twist*!

8 Magic Party for 7–9 year olds

If you decide to invite a magician to entertain your guests why not adopt the same theme for the rest of the party? We have recipes for magical food including a top-hat-and-rabbit birthday cake and ideas for decor that will give just the right atmosphere.

9 Hallowe'en Party for 7+ year olds

With additional atmosphere provided by hollowed-out turnips and pumpkins, paper bats and woollen cobwebs this is always a popular party. A cauldron of magic potions hubble-bubbling over a fire creates just the right note, even if it is a jam pan of fruit punch supported on three sticks and surrounded by red crepe paper!

10 Disco Party for Teenagers

Trying to strike a balance between older tastes and new-found sophistications can be rather trying; one popular answer is to try a simple warm buffet in the style of another country – choose from our French or Italian menus.

11　Bonfire Party for all ages

More and more families prefer to go to a properly organized bonfire party nowadays; not only is it much safer, the fireworks are better too! This is one children's party where the more adults there are present the better, and by arranging a combined effort among a group of friends or members of a street or sports club, the cost is spread more evenly.

The recipes in this section are given in quantities for 25 people, so to provide enough for 50 you just double the ingredients quantities. Everything listed is so easy that even a first-timer at group catering could cope with 100 guests, given some help!

1
Afternoon tea-party
for ten 1–2 year olds

The Organization

Your invitations to this party really need to include mummy or daddy as well as the child, since very few youngsters will be happy about being left at this age. (The recipe quantities allow for the extra guests.) A party of one and a half to two hours' duration will be quite long enough; it is far better for kids to be hectic for a short period and not to allow time for boredom to creep in.

You will need to assign a place for changing nappies and to set out cotton wool, tissues, cleanser and some disposable nappies ready for use. This will save time and fuss during the party should any of your guests need these items. It is also a good idea to put out one or two boxes of tissues in the room where the party is to be held. Excitement can provoke some strange reactions in small children!

Games aren't possible at this age. On hot days paddling pools and sandpits are the most popular areas of play especially when there are lots of small containers to empty and fill . . . a large pile of towels is essential!

If the party is to be held indoors, a quantity of large building bricks, shape sorters, cardboard boxes and tubes are always popular and can't really be spoilt even when bashed about!

Decorations for this party should be simple and colourful; balloons and twisted crepe paper streamers are excellent, and easy and quick to put up. The same shades of crepe paper could be used to cover the table. If you are able to fill the balloons with gas they can be secured to the

backs of the chairs around the table with string or used to provide a 'high-rise' table-centre decoration!

If the table stands on a carpet it is probably a good idea to run a sheet of thick polythene under it, but don't bother with this if the table is on a 'wipe-clean' surface – it's one less thing to trip over!

The Food

Potted beef playing-card sandwiches
Popular with adults and children alike, this potted beef is
equally good on sandwiches or hot toast. The cooking
time is long but with preparation and finishing taking
only 5 minutes., it is really worth making your own. It
will keep for up to a month in the fridge so can be made
well ahead if necessary.

Finnan haddock paste 'fishy' sandwiches
A very easy-to-make fish paste that is pleasantly mild and
creamy. It will keep for 2–3 days in the fridge and is
streets ahead of the bought variety.

Cream cheese and Marmite moon and star sandwiches
A lovely filling; good use of biscuit cutters adds an
interesting touch to an old tea-time favourite.

Baby fruit scones
Measuring only 3–4cm (1¼–1½in) across these are served
split and buttered, with separate bowls of jam and
whipped cream to hand. These little scones are especially
popular with visiting 'Mums'.

Small butterfly cakes and lemon frosties
Chocolate and vanilla flavoured butterflies and tiny sponge
cakes decorated with lemon icing are good choices for

'easy to eat' cakes and are not too rich for younger children.

The 1st (or 2nd) birthday cake
A very important cake, bound to appear in several photographs so it must be photogenic!

Our choice is a jolly-jelly-baby cake. Simplicity itself to make, it looks very bright and cheerful with its one or two candles burning brightly and provides just the right amount of wonder for a small child to take in!

The Drinks
Arrange to serve tea or coffee for the grown-up contingent and a light fruit juice (not blackcurrant, that's just asking for trouble) for the children.

Straws are popular but some of the younger guests may prefer plastic beakers. Paper cups are *not* a good idea for this age group since they don't react at all well to being grasped tightly!

Recipes

Potted beef

800g (2lb) lean topside of beef
¼ teaspoon grated nutmeg
good pinch of allspice
salt and freshly ground black pepper
150g (6oz) butter
1 small tin anchovies, well drained
milk
clarified butter, to seal (see below)

To make
1) Preheat the oven to 150°C (300°F) Gas Mark 2.
2) Sprinkle the beef with the spices and a little salt and pepper. Put into a casserole dish just big enough to hold it snugly.
3) Cut the butter into small pieces and place around the meat.
4) Place the casserole on the bottom shelf of the oven and cook for 5 hours. The meat should be almost falling apart.
5) While the beef cooks, place the drained anchovies in enough milk to cover them and soak for at least 1 hour. Drain and chop finely.
6) When the beef is cooked, drain it well in a colander until cold. Allow the butter to solidify in the casserole dish then gently lift it out.
7) Chop the meat into small pieces, discarding any gristle.

Add the anchovies and solidified butter and mince well. Check for seasoning.

8) Press the beef into small *clean* *ramekins, cover with clarified butter (see below) and keep cool.

* Because the length of time this beef can be kept is dependent on the cleanliness of its container. it is best to rinse the ramekins in boiling water *just* before using.

Clarified butter

Put 200g (8oz) butter into a small pan and melt over a low heat. As it melts the solids separate from the fat. Allow to cool slightly, then strain through muslin and discard the solids. Any left-over clarified butter will keep for 3–4 weeks in the fridge.

To make the potted beef sandwiches

1–2 ramekins potted beef
10 slices of bread, thinly cut
watercress to garnish

Because of the high butter content in the beef it is unnecessary to butter the bread first. Spread the potted beef thinly over the slices of bread. Place the slices together to make five sandwiches and then trim and cut each one into shapes about 3cm (1¼in) across. Small 'playing card' biscuit cutters are ideal for this purpose, but otherwise cut by hand, using a sharp knife, into diamonds, squares and triangles. Arrange on two plates with sprigs of watercress garnish, cover with clingfilm and store in a cool place until needed (not in the fridge, it makes the bread dry).
N.B. A little horseradish mixed with mustard goes very well in these sandwiches but is really only suitable for the grown-ups!

Finnan haddock paste

1 medium-sized fillet finnan haddock
2 tablespoons milk
100g (4oz) butter
½ teaspoon lemon juice
salt and freshly ground black pepper
clarified butter, to seal (see recipe for potted beef, page 16)

To make
1) Cook the haddock gently in the milk for 10 minutes. Drain and flake the fish. Discard any bones or skin.
2) Pound the fish and butter together with the lemon juice until smooth. This can be done either in a blender or food processor, or with a pestle and mortar.
3) Taste and add seasonings. Put into small ramekins and cover with clarified butter. Keep cool and use within 2–3 days.

To make the finnan haddock paste 'fishy' sandwiches

1–2 small ramekins finnan haddock paste
10 slices brown bread, cut thinly
cucumber slices and lemon wedges for garnish

As with the potted beef, the high butter content of the paste makes buttering the bread unnecessary.

Spread each slice of bread thinly with the paste and put the slices together to make five sandwiches. Trim and cut each one into 'fishy' shapes. No fish-shaped cutter? Try an inverted sherry glass to give a good round body to which you can attach a cucumber 'tail' and a tiny piece of peel for an eye. Arrange in shoals on two plates, garnish with small lemon wedges, and cover with clingfilm to keep fresh.

Cream cheese and Marmite moon and star sandwiches

100g (4oz) cream cheese
Marmite
10 slices of bread cut thinly
tomato wedges for garnish

To make

Spread each slice of bread with the cheese and smear just
the tiniest film of Marmite over five of the slices. Put the
pieces together to make five sandwiches. Trim and cut
each one into half-moon and star shapes, both of which
are fairly easy to do free hand with a sharp knife if you
cut out a small paper template first. Try to keep the size at
about 5cm (2in) across at the most.

Arrange the sandwiches on two plates and decorate
with the tomato wedges. Cover with clingfilm until
needed.

Baby fruit scones

400g (1lb) self-raising flour
1 teaspoon baking powder
1 level teaspoon salt
100g (4oz) butter
2 tablespoons caster sugar
100g (4oz) raisins or sultanas
2 eggs, beaten
15ml (¼pint) milk

To make

1) Preheat the oven to 230°C (450°F) Gas Mark 8.
2) Sift together the flour, baking powder and salt; rub in

the butter until the mixture looks like fine breadcrumbs.
3) Mix in the sugar and dried fruit then add most of the beaten egg and the milk. Knead together to a soft dough.
4) Turn on to a floured board and gently shape the dough into 'sausages' about 3–4cm (1¼–1½in) thick. Cut at 3cm (1¼in) intervals and put on to a greased baking sheet. Brush the tops lightly with the reserved beaten egg.
5) Place near the top of the oven and bake for 8–10 minutes. Turn on to a wire rack to cool.

To serve

Traditionally, fruit scones are served split and buttered, then filled with a good jam and whipped cream. This would be too rich for very young children so it would be best to split and butter the scones lightly, handing the jam and cream separately so that the 'grown-ups' can help themselves.

Small butterfly cakes and lemon frosties

200g (8oz) butter
200g (8oz) caster sugar
2 eggs, beaten
200g (8oz) self-raising flour
1 teaspoon cocoa (for the butterfly cakes)
½ teaspoon grated lemon rind (for the lemon frosties)

To make

1) Preheat the oven to 190°C (375°F) Gas Mark 5. Spread out 32 small paper baking cases on baking sheets.

2) Cream the butter and sugar together until light and fluffy.

3) Gradually add the beaten egg a little at a time, beating well between each addition.

4) Fold in the flour, using a metal spoon. Divide the mixture into two bowls; fold the cocoa into one half and the lemon rind into the other.

5) Spoon the mixtures separately into the baking cases, leaving space for the cakes to rise. Place in the oven and bake for 15–20 minutes. Allow to cool on a rack.

To finish the butterfly cakes

75g (3oz) butter
150g (6oz) icing sugar
2–3 drops vanilla essence

1) Cream the butter until light and fluffy, continue beating whilst adding the sugar a little at a time.

2) When all the sugar is absorbed, beat in the vanilla essence.

3) Scoop out a small circle from the top of each chocolate bun (a grapefruit knife is useful for this but is not essential). Fill in the space with some butter cream, either by piping or 'plopping' it on top. Cut the cake circle into two and set the pieces on to the butter cream to resemble wings. Dust with a little icing sugar.

To finish the lemon frosties

75g (3oz) butter
350g (12oz) icing sugar
3 tablespoons single cream
½ teaspoon grated lemon rind
2–3 lemon jelly sweets

1) Cream the butter until light and fluffy. Gradually add the sugar, cream and lemon rind, beating well between each addition.
2) Cover the top of each small lemon bun with the frosting then decorate with small pieces of lemon jelly sweets.

The 1st (or 2nd) birthday cake

200g (8oz) butter
200g (8oz) caster sugar
4 eggs, beaten
200g (8oz) self-raising flour
2 tablespoons apricot glaze (see below)

For the icing
50g (2oz) butter
4 tablespoons lemon juice
600g (1½lb) icing sugar
2–3 drops food colouring

For decoration
200–300g (8–12oz) jelly babies
candles and holders
small amount of royal icing (optional)

To make the cake
1) Preheat the oven to 180°C (350°F) Gas Mark 4. Grease and line two 20cm (8in) sandwich tins.
2) Cream the butter and sugar together until light and fluffy.
3) Gradually beat in the egg mixture a little at a time, then fold in the flour using a metal spoon.

4) Turn the mixture into the prepared cake tins and bake for 30–35 minutes. Cool on wire racks.

To make the apricot glaze

200g (8oz) apricot jam
2 tablespoons water

1) Melt the jam in the water in a small pan over a low heat. Push the purée through a sieve and return to the pan.
2) Bring to the boil and simmer gently until the mixture thickens slightly.

The glaze can be kept in a covered container for several weeks in the fridge or bottled like jam and stored in a cupboard.

To make the icing

1) Melt the butter over a low heat, stir in the lemon juice and one third of the icing sugar, continue stirring until the sugar dissolves.
2) When the mixture starts to simmer turn the heat up slightly and cook for just 2 minutes.
3) Take from the heat and beat in half the remaining sugar, add the food colouring to obtain whichever colour you have chosen, then beat in enough icing sugar to give a soft 'dough'.
4) Dust a board with icing sugar, turn out and knead the 'dough' until smooth. Keep, covered in clingfilm, until needed.

To finish the cake

1) Trim the cakes to give flat tops and bottoms. Sandwich together with a little warm apricot glaze.

2) Paint the top and sides of the cake with the warm glaze.

3) Turn the icing on to a board dusted with icing sugar and roll out thinly. Roll on to the top of the cake as though putting a lid on a pie.

4) Dust your hands with icing sugar and gently smooth and press the icing into place over the top and down the sides of the cake. Trim the bottom edge with a knife

5) To decorate, press the jelly babies around the sides of the cake and another circle of them around the top. Position the candle(s).

6) While it isn't really necessary to write the name of the child on the cake when he or she is this young, it does finish it off nicely. Use a small quantity of royal icing (or melted chocolate) and a No 2 writing nozzle.

Royal icing

 1 small egg white
 200g (8oz) icing sugar
 2–3 drops lemon juice
 ½ teaspoon glycerine, optional (use only when covering a cake with royal icing)

Beat the egg white until frothy. Gradually beat in the sugar, lemon juice and glycerine (if using). Continue beating until thick and smooth. Cover with a damp cloth and allow to stand for several hours.

2
Teddy-bear's Picnic
for eight 2–5 year olds

The Organization

The basic requirements for this party are the same as for the 1st (or 2nd) birthday. You may need to allocate a nappy-changing area and will definitely need lots of moist tissues! Some parents will prefer to stay with their offspring, and one and a half hours should be long enough for everyone.

Invitations can be teddy-shaped and should include the child and his or her favourite bear. Plan the party for outdoors with a picnic on the lawn and cross your fingers that the weather will be kind. If it does rain the only necessary change, apart from the location of the tablecloth, will be in the choice of suitable toys for the children to play with.

Arranged games won't be possible but you could organize a teddy hunt, providing that the cardboard teddies are placed where toddlers can pick them up easily. They can look really effective and provide lots of fun, strategically placed to peep around trees and bushes.

Tricycles, see-saws and a good selection of push-along toys will all be put to good use. Try to borrow one or two extra-large toys so that you don't have much of a problem with all the children wanting to play with the same toy at the same time.

Even if the weather has been dry for a while it will still be a good idea to put a ground sheet under trvelling rugs for sitting on. Choose the brightest checked tablecloth you can find and anchor it well at each corner. Plastic cups and double the normal quantity of paper napkins will be needed.

Outside, balloons will be more trouble than they're worth, since they tend to burst or float away and the resulting crescendo of 'wahs' is to be avoided at all costs! Bunting or flags would provide good outside decoration, but this is one party where it isn't really essential.

The Food

Crunchy chicken drumsticks
Using crushed cornflakes in place of breadcrumbs gives these chicken legs a lovely flavour.

Picnic kebabs
An easy way to serve all the favourite party bits and pieces. These kebabs combine crisp bacon rolls, cheese, pineapple and, yes, those inevitable sausages.

Meat Loaf
This meat loaf isn't too highly spiced and so is very popular with younger children.

Soft white rolls – split and buttered; crisps; and a selection of vegetable sticks – celery, carrot, etc, are all that is needed with these dishes.

Little trifles
Made up in small paper trifle cases, these desserts are usually just the right amount for young children.

Jam-filled Swiss roll
There's always a fascination about food you can 'play' with, and there's nothing quite like a slice of Swiss roll, unravelled and eaten as though it was a long worm!

Sponge finger biscuits
A lovely homemade biscuit, served plain for the children, or dipped in chocolate and sandwiched together with cream for grown-ups.

Teddy-bear birthday cake

A smashing cake for little children. The teddy bear is shaped in relief and decorated with butter-cream 'fur'.

Recipes

CRUNCHY CHICKEN DRUMSTICKS

1 teaspoon salt
½ teaspoon pepper
75g (3oz) flour
16 chicken drumsticks
3 eggs, beaten
400g (1lb) cornflakes, crushed
oil for frying
cutlet frills and lemon wedges to garnish

To make

1) Mix together the salt, pepper and flour. Skin the drumsticks then roll them in the flour. Tap away any excess flour then dip each drumstick in the beaten egg mixture to coat well.
2) Roll the drumsticks in the crushed cornflakes until well covered. Chill for at least 30 minutes.
3) Pour the oil into a deep pan to a depth of 8cm (3in). Heat to 160° (325°F) and fry the chicken legs, 3 or 4 at a time, for about 10 minutes or until cooked through and golden brown. Drain on kitchen paper and set aside to cool.
4) Pop the cutlet frills on to the legs just before serving and garnish with lemon wedges.

PICNIC KEBABS

400g (1lb) pork sausages
200g (8oz) streaky bacon
200g (8oz) mild Cheddar cheese
1 large tin pineapple chunks
skewers and cocktail sticks

To make

1) Grill the sausages until golden brown on all sides. Put aside to cool.
2) Derind the bacon and cut into short strips some 6cm (2½in) long. Roll up each strip and secure with a cocktail stick. Grill until crisp and brown. Put aside to cool. Take out the sticks.
3) Chop the cheese into small dice. Drain the pineapple well.
4) Assemble the kebabs using the pineapple chunks to separate the cheese from the meats.

MEAT LOAF

50g (2oz) onion, finely chopped
rind of ½ lemon, grated
400g (1lb) lean beef ⎫
200g (8oz) lean pork ⎬ minced well
200g (8oz) lean bacon ⎭
50g (2oz) breadcrumbs
½ teaspoon sage
1 good teaspoon salt
freshly ground black pepper
1 teaspoon Worcestershire sauce
2 eggs

To make

1) Preheat the oven to 170°C (325°F) Gas Mark 3. Put all the dry ingredients and the Worcestershire sauce into a large bowl and mix together well.
2) Beat the eggs and use to bind the ingredients together. Turn the mixture into a loaf tin, cover with foil and bake for 1½ hours. Remove the foil and bake for a further 30 minutes.
3) Pour off the fat and allow the loaf to cool. Serve cut into slices (with a good chutney) for the adults and cubed on sticks (with tomato sauce) for the children.

LITTLE TRIFLES

1 packet trifle sponges
12–16 paper trifle cases
1 packet raspberry jelly
600ml (1pint) custard
150ml (¼pint) cream
sugar strands to decorate

To make

1) Split the sponges between the trifle cases. Make up the red jelly and pour over the sponges. Put to one side until set.
2) Pour over just enough custard to cover and when completely cool decorate with whipped cream and sugar strands.

JAM-FILLED SWISS ROLL

100g (4oz) caster sugar
3 large eggs
100g (4oz) plain flour
1 tablespoon hot water
caster sugar ⎱
raspberry jam ⎰ for the filling

To make

1) Preheat the oven to 220°C (425°F) Gas Mark 7. Grease and line a large Swiss roll tin – 30 × 23cm (12 × 9in) – with non-stick paper.
2) Using an electric mixer, beat the sugar and eggs together in a large bowl until the mixture is thick and creamy. (If you haven't a mixer, simply place the bowl over a pan of hot water and use a whisk.)
3) Sift the flour in two or three stages, folding in with a large metal spoon; fold in the hot water gently.
4) Turn the mixture into the prepared tin and bake for 7–10 minutes until golden brown and risen.
5) Spread a damp tea-towel on a working surface. Cover with a piece of greaseproof paper and sprinkle with caster sugar.
6) Take the cake from the oven and turn out on top of the sugared paper. Trim the edges and peel off the lining paper.
7) Warm the jam slightly then spread it over the cake. Roll up, using the greaseproof paper to help with handling and try to form an evenly shaped roll.
8) Cut on the diagonal in thin slices and arrange on a plate.

SPONGE FINGER BISCUITS *(makes approximately 30 biscuits)*

3 large eggs
75g (3oz) caster sugar
1–2 drops vanilla essence
75g (3oz) flour
1 large forcing bag and plain tube, 1cm (½in) diameter
melted chocolate, cream, jam for finishing (optional)

To make

1) Preheat the oven to 170°C (325°F) Gas Mark 3. Grease a baking sheet with butter.
2) Separate the eggs and whisk the yolks with the sugar until light and fluffy. Add the vanilla essence.
3) Beat the egg whites until very stiff then fold into the egg yolk mixture with the flour.
4) Put the mixture into the forcing bag and pipe strips 8cm (3in) long on to the baking sheet. Bake for 20 minutes but do not allow to brown. Cool on a wire rack.
5) The biscuits are delicious just as they are, but should you wish to decorate them simply dip the end into melted chocolate and sandwich two biscuits together with jam or cream (or even both).

TEDDY-BEAR BIRTHDAY CAKE

The teddy is made by using two round sponge cakes and one slab cake which is cut up to give feet, arms and ears. Any left-over cake can be used in the little trifles.

300g (12oz) butter
300g (12oz) caster sugar
6 eggs
300g (12oz) self-raising flour
3 tablespoons hot water
1 round deep cake tin 18cm (7in) diameter
1 round deep cake tin, 12cm (5in) diameter
1 square cake tin, 20cm (8in)
1 very large cake board, at least 40cm (16in) square
4–5 tablespoons apricot glaze (see page 22)

To make

1) Preheat the oven to 180°C (350°F) Gas Mark 4. Grease and line the baking tins.
2) Cream the butter and sugar together until light and fluffy. Beat in the eggs, one at a time, making sure the mixture is well blended after each addition.
3) Sift the flour and fold into the mixture with a metal spoon. Stir in the hot water. Divide the mixture between the prepared cake tins.
4) Bake the two smaller cakes for 45 minutes, the large cake for 1¼ hours. Cool on a rack.
5) Position the two circular cakes on the board to form the teddy's head and body. Cut arms, legs and ears from the slab cake.
6) Put the cut pieces of cake into position on the board, warm the apricot glaze then brush all over the cake.

To finish the cake

piping bags and a rose tube
vanilla butter cream made with 400g (1lb) icing sugar
   (see method on page 20)
1–2 drops food colouring
2 green Smarties

ribbon
candles and holders

1) Pipe small rosettes of buttercream all over the teddy, leaving his feet and paw pads plain.
2) Mix a suitably contrasting 1–2 drops of food colouring into a small amount of butter cream and use to pipe small rosettes over the plain parts. You could also use the contrasting colour for the mouth, nose and ears.
3) Use the Smarties for eyes and tie the ribbon into a bow before securing it on the teddy's neck. Position the candles on the bear's tummy.

3
'Our Most Favourite Things' Party
for twelve 4–6 year olds

The Organization

Send out invitations 10–14 days before the party is to take place, remembering particularly to specify how long the party will last (two hours is ample), and whether play or party clothes should be worn.

Some 4–6 year olds are a little vague about who to ask to their party, so it is usually a good idea to check with their form teacher or play-school organizer to make sure that all particular friends are included.

It is essential to keep 4–6 year olds occupied all of the time, otherwise the boys have fights and the girls get peevish! The most critical time is as other guests are arriving and cards and presents are being opened by the birthday girl or boy. According to the poll of most favourite things, a treasure hunt is the best way to keep children busy while you take the coats, point out the way to the bathroom and toilet and enthuse over the presents! For the details of this and all the other most popular games, please turn to the special 'games' chapter, page 173.

A bran tub of prizes is the 'tops'! The children win tokens during the party to exchange for a dip in the tub after tea. Do make absolutely sure that each child 'wins' at least one token by the end of the party. Tokens can be anything you have available; empty cotton reels are particularly good and you can write the winner's name on them in felt-tip to prevent confusion later on.

The most favourite prizes are small boxes of chocolate beans and fun-sized chocolate bars, or pencil sharpeners, erasers and small magnifying glasses. All of which should

be properly wrapped-up – our panel members were most specific about this!

For decorations, balloons are the first favourite followed by fairy lights. Special party-sets of paper plates, napkins and tablecloths were all given the thumbs up, although each child had a different favourite design!

Party hats are popular, the substantial variety being much preferred to the paper ones found in crackers.

It is a good idea to have a box of moist tissues handy and a box or two of ordinary tissues placed at strategic intervals won't go amiss either!

The Food

No surprises on this part of our poll. For most children the food is very secondary to the games, but even so the same items appeared time and again on their lists.

Cheese and sausage hedgehogs
One of *the* most popular dishes. The cheese can be garnished with tiny silverskin onions or pineapple chunks, and the sausages with gherkins or beetroot.

Sausage rolls
Small sausage rolls served just warm with melt-in-the mouth pastry and a good flavoured sausage-meat are also popular with adults. Try to keep some back for collecting parents to nibble while the children are putting on their coats.

Crudités
Described in an amazing number of ways on our lists, the combination of tasty dips and raw cut vegetables is clearly very popular. Crisps, cheese straws and tiny savoury biscuits are all popular 'dunkers' too.

Filled rolls
Soft bridge rolls filled with boiled ham and sliced tomato or chopped egg – but *no* cress – were outright winners of the 'sandwich' award.

Knickerbocker glories
Stripy jelly and fruit and custard concoctions were mentioned in everyone's list. Most children felt that some sort of outlandish jelly dish was essential even if they don't like jelly themselves!

Ice cream
A most popular sweet, it can be served with a chocolate or raspberry sauce, but our panel felt it really must have crisp wafer biscuits to be 'right'!

Train and tender birthday cake
The old favourite chocolate Swiss roll train cake came out on top, even with the girls! It is very easy to make and always looks extra-special.

Our instructions are for a train and fire tender, into which can be placed several small dolls, teddies or soldiers which makes it just a little bit different. Another fun idea is to fill the tender with tiny parcels, one for each child. A piece of chunky chocolate is about the right size for this.

The drinks
The most favourite drink was fresh orange juice mixed with lemonade and served with an ice cube, two straws and a twist of orange or lemon peel! Thank goodness no one said they preferred this cocktail 'shaken, but not stirred'!

Recipes

CHEESE AND SAUSAGE HEDGEHOGS
(makes 2)

200g (8oz) miniature chipolata sausages
400g (1lb) mild Cheddar cheese
1 small can pineapple chunks
1 small jar silverskin onions
1 small jar gherkins
3–4 small pickled beetroot
2 large grapefruit
aluminium foil
cocktail sticks (wooden ones are best)

To make

1) Grill the sausages until golden brown on all sides. Allow to cool.
2) Cut the cheese into cubes 2cm (¾in) square.
3) Drain the pineapple chunks, onions and gherkins. Cut the beetroot in half.
4) Cover each grapefruit in foil then start to assemble the hedgehogs.
5) Thread an onion, a piece of cheese and a pineapple chunk on to a cocktail stick and press together gently then spear the other end of the stick into the grapefruit. Continue doing this until the 'quills' are quite dense, interspacing the cheese sticks with ones made up from sausages with either gherkins or beetroot halves. Make up the second 'hedgehog'.

N.B. There are several alternatives to the 'grapefruit in foil' base. Lemon 'pigs' are made from good oval-shaped lemons with cocktail sticks for legs, cloves for eyes and a little nifty scoring to produce a curly tail. Cucumber 'crocodiles' can be made from a whole cucumber cut horizontally up to one third of the way through, with 'V'-shaped cuts to represent teeth, the jaws then propped open with a cocktail stick. Very popular with the boys! To finish him off, insert two clove eyes and a thin strip of red pepper tongue.

Large potatoes can also be a good base, but they do look better covered.

SAUSAGE ROLLS

200g (8oz) plain flour
pinch of salt
150g (6oz) butter (chilled)
½ teaspoon lemon juice
water to mix
½ teaspoon dried mixed herbs
1 tablespoon grated onion
400g (1lb) sausagemeat
salt and freshly ground black pepper
1 egg, beaten

To make
1) Sift the flour and salt into a bowl. Cut the butter into small cubes about 2cm (¾in) square. Add to the flour.
2) Carefully mix into a stiff dough using the lemon juice and about 4 tablespoons of cold water.
3) Turn the pastry on to a lightly floured board and roll out

into a rectangle. Fold over into three then turn through 90°. Repeat this rolling out and folding and turning three times. Cover and allow to rest for 30 minutes.

4) Mix the herbs and grated onion with the sausagemeat and season lightly.
5) Preheat the oven to 220°C (425°F) Gas Mark 7.
6) Roll the pastry out very thinly and cut into strips about 10cm (4in) wide.
7) Divide the sausagemeat between the pastry strips and run a roll of the meat mixture (about 2.5cm (1in) in diameter) down the centre of each one.
8) Brush one side of the pastry with some beaten egg, roll the pastry over the top of the meat and seal. Position the sealed edge at the bottom. Press down lightly.
9) Decorate by snipping little 'V' shapes with scissors all along the roll.
10) Cut into rolls 4cm (1½in) long, place on greased baking sheets and bake for 20–25 minutes, until the pastry is golden brown.

To serve

Sausage rolls are best served warm. Don't try to keep them warm for a long period of time though; it is better to allow them to cool then re-heat when needed.

CRUDITÉS – THE DIPS

Green dip

4 tablespoons mayonnaise
1 tablespoon mint sauce
1 tablespoon natural yoghurt
1 teaspoon freshly chopped parsley

Stir all the ingredients together until well mixed, sprinkle with a little more chopped parsley.

Tomato dip

4 tablespoons mayonnaise
2 teaspoons tomato purée
1 tablespoon natural yoghurt
a little paprika pepper to garnish

Stir the mayonnaise, purée and yoghurt together until well mixed. Sprinkle with a little paprika pepper before serving.

Cheese dip

1 small packet cream cheese
2 tablespoons natural yoghurt
salt and freshly ground black pepper

Mash the cheese and yoghurt together with a fork until creamy and smooth. Season to taste.

Cucumber dip

½ cucumber
150ml (¼pint) natural yoghurt
½ teaspoon mild curry powder

Peel and grate the cucumber. Mix together with the yoghurt and curry powder. Chill before using.

CRUDITÉS – THE VEGETABLES

Choose any vegetables that will stay crisp when cut. Carrots, peppers, celery, cucumber, radishes, and small cauliflower florets are most suitable.

Cut the carrots, peppers, celery and cucumber into long matchsticks about 5cm (2in) long by 1cm (¼in) thick and arrange around a dip with crisps, small savoury biscuits and cheese straws.

CHEESE STRAWS

100g (4oz) plain flour
salt
Cayenne pepper
50g (2oz) butter
50g (2oz) Cheddar cheese
1 egg yolk
water to mix

To make

1) Preheat the oven to 200°C (400°F) Gas Mark 6.
2) Sift the flour into a bowl with a pinch of salt and Cayenne pepper.
3) Cut the butter into small pieces and rub into the flour until the mixture resembles fine breadcrumbs. Grate in the cheese.
4) Mix into a stiffish dough using the egg yolk and enough cold water to bind the ingredients together.
5) Turn on to a lightly floured board and roll out to 0.05cm (¼in) thick. Cut into straws about 8cm (3in) long by 0.05cm (¼in) thick. Brush one or two straws with water on one end. Form into 'O' shapes and seal.
6) Place on a greased baking-sheet and cook for 10–12 minutes until light brown and crisp.

To serve

Put several straws through each 'ring' to hold them

together neatly. Leave plain when using with a dip, but sprinkle with a little paprika pepper on the ends for other occasions.

KNICKERBOCKER GLORIES

1 packet raspberry jelly
1 packet lime jelly
1 large tin fruit salad
300 ml (½pint) custard sauce (cold)
150ml (¼pint) double cream
glacé cherries, for decoration

To make
1) Make up the raspberry jelly and allow to cool.
2) Drain the fruit salad and put a dessertspoonful of the fruit into the bottom of each tall sundae glass. Pour over enough raspberry jelly to cover and put into the fridge to set., Keep any left–over jelly to one side.
3) Make up the lime jelly and allow to cool. Place in the fridge until almost at setting point.
4) Whisk the lime jelly until smooth and frothy. Pour a layer of this whisked jelly over the set layer of fruit and jelly in each sundae glass. Return to the fridge to set the new layer.
5) In a bowl, mix any remaining frothy jelly with the rest of the fruit. Placc the bowl in the fridge until contents are set.
6) Roughly chop up the left–over raspberry jelly and the lime/fruit jelly. Put a layer of custard into each sundae glass followed by layers of chopped jellies.
7) Whip the cream and pipe a rosette on top of each sundae. Decorate each with a glacé cherry.

Alternative fillings

The basic jelly layers with ice-cream between the set and the chopped jellies and topped with cream and raspberry sauce is a very popular filling – but, of course, it has to be assembled just before serving because of the ice-cream.

ICE-CREAM WITH CHOCOLATE OR RASPBERRY SAUCE

1 large carton vanilla ice-cream (easy scoop is best for a party)

Chocolate sauce

100g (4oz) dark chocolate
25g (1oz) butter
2 drops vanilla essence
4 tablespoons milk

1) Melt the chocolate and butter together in a basin positioned over a pan of hot water. Stir until smooth.
2) Add the vanilla essence and milk and stir gently until completely blended.

This sauce is best served warm. It is delicious when a few chopped walnuts are added, but most children prefer it without.

Raspberry sauce

200g (8oz) raspberries (fresh, or frozen and defrosted)
icing sugar to taste

1) Push the raspberries through a sieve, using the back of a spoon to make sure as much juice as possible is extracted.
2) Whisk in about 2 teaspoons of icing sugar, or more if the sauce is too tart. Continue whisking until the sugar is dissolved. Chill until needed.

TRAIN AND TENDER BIRTHDAY CAKE

For the 'train' cake

3 eggs
100g (4oz) caster sugar
100g (4oz) plain flour
1 tablespoon hot water
3 tablespoons apricot glaze (see page 22)

1) Preheat the oven to 220°C (425°F) Gas Mark 7. Line a Swiss roll tin 30 × 23cm (12 × 9in) with non-stick paper.
2) Put the eggs and sugar into a large bowl and beat with an electric whisk until pale and thick and the mixture leaves a trail when the whisk is lifted. (This can be done in a bowl placed over hot water if an ordinary whisk is used.)
3) Sift the flour on to the mixture then fold in, using a large metal spoon. Stir in the hot water.
4) Turn the mixture into the prepared tin, level off and bake for 7–10 minutes until golden brown and risen.
5) Place a clean tea-towel wrung out in warm water on a work surface and smooth out. Cover with a sheet of greaseproof paper and sprinkle the paper lightly with caster sugar.

6) Turn the cake out on to the paper. Peel off the non-stick paper and brush the top generously with apricot glaze.

7) Roll up, using the greaseproof paper to help with handling and try to achieve a uniform roll. Set the cake to one side.

For the 'tender' cake

200g (8oz) self-raising flour
1 heaped teaspoon baking powder
pinch of salt
200g (8oz) soft margarine
200g (8oz) caster sugar
4 large eggs

1) Preheat the oven to 170°C (325°F) Gas Mark 3. Grease and line a 20cm (8in) square cake tin.

2) Sift the flour, baking powder and salt into a large bowl. Add the margarine, sugar and eggs and beat using an electric beater until the mixture is completely smooth.

3) Turn the mixture into the prepared cake tin and bake for 30–40 minutes in the centre of the oven. Remove from the oven and leave to cool in the tin.

For the chocolate icing

150g (6oz) dark chocolate
15g (½oz) butter
400g (1lb) icing sugar
water to mix

1) Melt the chocolate in 2 tablespoons of water over a low heat. Stir in the butter. Allow to cool slightly.

2) Gradually beat in the icing sugar a spoonful at a time,

adding a little more water if necessary. Allow to stand for 30 minutes then stir well to get rid of any air bubbles.

To finish the cake

1 swiss roll
1 square cake
chocolate icing
vanilla-flavoured butter cream, using 100g (4oz) butter
  (see method, page 20)
piping bags, small rose nozzle
candles, holders and two red Smarties
cottonwool

1) Cut four slices 2cm (¾in) thick from the Swiss roll. Cut each of these in half to form the wheels. Put the remaining Swiss roll and the wheels on to a wire rack and coat with the chocolate icing.
2) Cut a square piece 12 × 5cm (5 × 2in) wide from the plain cake. Stand on end on the wire rack and coat with the icing. Cut the remaining cake into three rectangles to form a tender leaving a gap in the middle for the toys and parcels. Finally cut a small round piece of cake for the funnel. Put all these pieces on to the wire rack and coat with chocolate icing.
3) When the icing is set, sandwich the pieces of train and tender together with some butter cream onto the board the cake will be served from.
4) Pop a small rosette nozzle into a piping bag and fill with butter cream. Pipe small rosettes around each join, the edges and insides of the wheels and top of the funnel. Write the child's name on the side of the cab in small rosettes, position the candles and put the toys or little parcels into the tender.
5) Finish by putting two Smartie 'lights' at the front and a little puff of cottonwool on the funnel for 'smoke'.

4
Cowboy Party
for twelve 4–6 year olds

The Organization

Try to carry the Western theme on through every aspect of the party. Invitations can easily be made cowboy-shaped with the aid of a piece of tracing paper and the wording could make good use of some of the more well-known cowboy phrases! Do make sure that it is clear that your guests are to be in fancy dress; check shirts, jeans and a hat are really all that's needed, but gun belts and masks will appear like magic!

A party lasting for not more than two hours is best for children of this age and it is important to keep them 'on the go' the whole time. A game of 'hunt the Indian' played while guests are arriving is a good idea and the children could gather 'notches' on their belts or holsters to

exchange for small prizes before going home. Another idea for prize tokens could be small stick-on feathers for their hats.

A red and white gingham tablecloth will give just the right effect for the 'chuck-wagon'-style food, while home-made totem poles and tee-pees along with 'Wanted' posters and other 'Wells Fargo' items will help create the atmosphere of the Wild West.

Try to choose games that are easy to adopt to the cowboy theme. 'Pin the tail on the donkey' becomes 'Pin the star on the sheriff' and games that need music such as 'musical statues' or 'pass the parcel' work well when played to some fast guitar-picking or fiddle-playing.

As with all children's parties have boxes of tissues and sponge cloths at the ready; one or two of the guests are bound to be a little too quick on the draw!

The Food

Bacon, sausages and baked beans are absolutely essential to the wellbeing of cowboys! The rest of the dishes suggested for this party have a distinct American flavour and keep the basic theme of the party going throughout the meal.

Bacon and sausage kebab
The easiest way to grill bacon and sausages for twelve and to ensure that it is all ready at the same time.

Hash brown potatoes
An adaptation of the popular fried potato dish. In this case it is cooked in the oven.

American pancakes
Traditionally served with maple syrup or blueberry jam and bacon. Most British children prefer them served after the savoury course. This recipe can be cooked well before the pancakes are needed and re-heated in the oven.

Strawberry shortcakes
A delicious sweet, the combination of soft fruit, cream and shortcake is also popular with grownups. Try to save a few for collecting parents to enjoy.

Chocolate brownies and peanut cookies
Anyone who has watched American films could be forgiven for thinking that the only things the children eat at

home are chocolate brownies and peanut cookies – here
are the reasons why!

Wagon train birthday cake

The cowboy's birthday cake is made so that there is a
'covered wagon' for each guest. Clever use of small plastic
cowboys and Indians creates an exciting scene that is a
good finishing touch.

The Drinks

Sarsaparilla should be the first choice, but in terms of
popularity perhaps Coca-cola or 7-up would be much
better choices. Milk shakes or a still orange could be
offered to children who don't care for fizzy drinks.

Recipes

BACON AND SAUSAGE KEBABS

12 rashers bacon
48 cocktail-sized chipolata sausages
12 skewers, about 15cm (6in) long
12 medium-sized tomatoes

To make
1) Trim the rind from the bacon and then cut each rasher into 3 or 4 pieces. Roll up each piece.
2) Thread the sausages and bacon rolls alternately on to the skewers.
3) Pre-heat the grill for 5 minutes. Grill the kebabs for 2–3 minutes then push the tomatoes on to the skewers. Continue grilling until the sausages are golden brown and the bacon crisp.

To serve
Slide the bacon, sausage and tomato from each skewer on to a plate before serving. This will avoid any mishaps with hot skewers which could result in tears.

HASH BROWN POTATOES

1.2kg (3lb) potatoes
200g (8oz) streaky bacon

50g (2oz) butter
salt

To make

1) Peel the potatoes and cut into quarters. Bring to the boil in some lightly salted water and simmer until almost cooked. Drain well and leave to cool. Cut into dice about 2cm (¾in) square.
2) Preheat the oven to 190°C (375°F) Gas Mark 5.
3) Trim the rind from the bacon and cut into small pieces. Cook over a low heat in its own fat in a large flameproof casserole dish until crisp.
4) Add the butter to the bacon and its fat and when sizzling put in the potatoes. Brown on all sides then put the casserole uncovered into the oven. Bake for 20–30 minutes. Drain on kitchen paper, then serve straight away.

AMERICAN PANCAKES

125g (5oz) plain flour
good pinch of salt
3 eggs
225ml (⅜pint) milk
3 tablespoons cold water
30g (1½oz) melted butter
25g (1oz) butter melted in 1 tablespoon vegetable oil, for frying

To make

1) If you have a blender or food processor, simply put all the pancake ingredients into the bowl and blend well.
2) To mix by hand, sift the flour and salt into a bowl, add

the eggs and gradually pour in the milk and water,
stirring all the time to mix. Beat the batter well until
there are no lumps and then add the cooled melted
butter.

3) Allow to stand for 1–2 hours in the fridge.

4) Heat a 12cm (5in) diameter frying pan to the point
where a drop of water splashed on to it evaporates
immediately. Brush with the butter/oil mixture then
pour in about 2 tablespoons of batter. Tilt the pan this
way and that so that the batter runs around and covers
the base. When just setting flip over and cook the
other side.

5) Cook all the pancakes in this way, piling them neatly
on top of each other on a heatproof plate. Re-heat
when needed by covering the pancakes with foil and
popping the dish into a warm oven for about 10–15
minutes. Separate carefully and serve with melted
butter and maple syrup or blueberry jam (bilberry jam
is probably the nearest to this).

STRAWBERRY SHORTCAKES

400g (1lb) self-raising flour
2 level teaspoons baking powder
½ level teaspoon salt
150g (8oz) butter, chilled
150g (8oz) sugar
2 eggs
milk to mix

For finishing

400g (1lb) strawberries
2–3 tablespoons caster sugar
150ml (¼ pint) double cream

To make

1) Preheat the oven to 190°C (375°F) Gas Mark 5.
2) Sift the flour, baking powder and salt together into a large mixing bowl. Cut the butter into small pieces and rub in until the mixture resembles fine bread-crumbs. Mix in the sugar.
3) Beat the eggs and use to bind the dry ingredients together into a soft dough. Add a little milk if necessary.
4) Turn the dough on to a lightly floured board and knead gently until smooth.
5) Roll out the dough and cut out small rounds 5cm (2in) in diameter. Put on to a greased baking tray and bake for 20 minutes, or until firm and golden. Cool on a wire rack.
6) Prepare the strawberries, then set aside enough whole fruits to decorate the top of each shortcake. Halve the rest and sprinkle with caster sugar to taste.
7) Whip up the cream until stiff. Split each shortcake in half and fill with a blob of cream and some strawberry halves. Sandwich together and pipe a small cream whirl on each cake finishing off with a whole strawberry in the centre.

CHOCOLATE BROWNIES

50g (2oz) dark chocolate
100g (4oz) caster sugar
100g (4oz) butter
2 eggs
50g (2oz) plain flour
½ level teaspoon baking powder
½ level teaspoon salt

2–3 drops vanilla essence
100g (4oz) chopped roasted hazelnuts

To make
1) Pre-heat the oven to 180°C (350°F) Gas Mark 4. Grease a 20cm (8in) square cake tin.
2) Melt the chocolate in a bowl placed over a pan of hot water. Set aside to cool.
3) Cream the sugar and butter together in a large bowl until light and fluffy.
4) Beat in the eggs and the chocolate. When well blended sift in the flour, baking powder and salt. Beat well then stir in the vanilla essence and the nuts.
5) Pour the mixture into the cake tin and bake for 30–40 minutes. Cool for several minutes then cut into 5cm (2in) squares.

PEANUT COOKIES

100g (4oz) peanut butter
100g (4oz) butter
100g (4oz) sugar
100g (4oz) dark brown sugar
1 egg, beaten
good pinch of salt
125g (5oz) plain flour
½ level teaspoon baking powder
¼ level teaspoon bicarbonate of soda

To make
1) Preheat the oven to 180°C (350°F) Gas Mark 4.
2) In a bowl, cream the peanut butter, the butter and the two sugars until the mixture is light and fluffy.

3) Beat in the egg then fold in the flour, salt, baking powder and bicarbonate of soda. Mix to a smooth stiff dough. Chill for 30 minutes.
4) Roll out the dough on a floured board and cut into 5cm (2in) diameter rounds. Place on a greased baking tray and cook for 10–15 minutes. Cool on a wire rack.

WAGON TRAIN BIRTHDAY CAKE

The finished cake should look like a series of covered wagons (one for each child) arranged in a circle as though withstanding an Indian attack. Some small sets of cowboy and cavalry figures are used to create the excitement and a large round cake with the centre removed and cut up to form the wagon tops is used for the base.

For the cake

200g (8oz) butter
200g (8oz) caster sugar
4 eggs
2–3 drops vanilla essence
200g (8oz) self-raising flour

1) Preheat the oven to 180°C (350°F) Gas Mark 4. Grease and line a 25cm (10in) round cake tin.
2) Cream the butter and sugar together in a large bowl until light and fluffy. Beat in the eggs one at a time; when well mixed add the vanilla essence.
3) Sift the flour then fold into the mixture until thoroughly absorbed. Turn into the prepared cake tin and bake for 35–40 minutes. Turn on to a wire rack to cool.

For the moulding icing

Two separate lots of this icing are needed; one to be left white for the wagon tops and the other coloured to use for the wagon bottoms.

2 egg whites
2 heaped tablespoons liquid glucose
800g (2lb) icing sugar
1–2 drops food colouring

1) Mix the egg whites and glucose together with a fork in a large bowl.
2) Add the icing sugar a little at a time and mix until a stiff dough is formed. (You may need slightly more or less icing sugar dependent on the size of the eggs).
3) Divide the dough into two portions and add the food colouring to one half. Place each piece in turn on a flat working surface dusted with cornflour and knead until smooth.
4) Cover with clingfilm until needed. This icing will keep for up to a month in the fridge.

To finish the cake

1 × 25cm (10in) round cake
white moulding icing
coloured moulding icing
2–3 tablespoons apricot glaze (warmed) (see page 22)
butter cream made with 100g/4oz butter and coloured green (see page 20)
3 tablespoons coconut, coloured green
candles and holders
plastic horses (1 per wagon)
small round 'iced gem' biscuits (4 per wagon) to use as wheels

small rose piping tube and bags
large cake board, 40cm (16in) square, or larger
edible food colouring pen (to write the children's names
    on the wagons)
a quantity of marauding Indians, brave homesteaders
    and dashing cavalry!

1) Cut a circle 20cm (8in) in diameter from the centre of
the cake. Position the remaining ring slightly to one
side of the cake board.

2) Using a sharp knife cut out gaps between the number
of wagons required, leaving the cake about 3cm (1in)
high at its lowest points. (At this stage the ring should
look rather like the top of a battlement.)

3) Brush the ring with warmed apricot glaze. Pipe
green buttercream over the ground surface of the
cake and board and sprinkle with coconut. Cover
the wagon bases with coloured moulding icing,
smoothing it gently into place with your hands. Stick
the biscuit wheels in place with a little buttercream.

4) Cut up the centre of the cake to form the wagon tops.
(The curved edge will be used as the top of each
wagon). Cut each piece into a thick wedge shape and
level off to form the bottom edge.

5) Brush each wagon top with apricot glaze and cover
with some white moulding icing, again smoothing it
into place with your hands.

6) Decorate by cutting a 'frill' into the icing at the front
and back of each wagon and then write the child's
name on top with the special pen (or pipe the name on
using melted chocolate).

7) Position the wagon tops on the bases, securing with a
little apricot glaze. Put the candles and holders on to
the wagon of the 'birthday boy' (or 'girl').

8) Finish off by arranging a scene of blood-curdling
authenticity around the wagons using the little figures!

If you want to make a campfire in the centre of the scene, this can be achieved using red Smarties and Matchmakers!

5
Fairy Princess Party
for ten 4–7 year olds

The Organization

Everything about this party should be as over-the-top pretty-pretty as can be! Start by edging the invitations in silver, write the wording in gold, and then cover the lot with glitter!!

The table should be a masterpiece of overstatement; covered with tinsel-edged white crepe paper and decorated with leaves sprayed gold and silver, an arrangement of which placed over a mirror and used as the centrepiece will look super. Twinkling fairy lights and some Christmas decorations could also be used to great effect.

This is definitely the party at which to show off a pretty dress. However, even if you try to choose games that

don't involve lying down on the floor or anything too hectic, the fact remains that whilst a few little girls can walk through a coal mine and come out looking pristine, most of them need less than five minutes to get positively grubby. How they will look after a two-hour party is anybody's guess!

Again it is best to adapt the games being played to fit the party's theme. In this case you could start with 'Find the fairies' wands' (made from straws and cardboard) then go on to a game of 'Cinderella's slipper'. Coronets and tiaras are very easy to make and could be the basis of a game where each child tries to find a crown made just for him or her.

The success of this party depends to some extent on the amount of ingenuity and imagination put into planning it, but sadly there seems to be no way of getting your three wishes granted in time to help with the clearing-up!

The Food

Food for this party is light, delicate and very pretty. Some dishes may seem a little luxurious but the portions are small and after all you are feeding 'royalty'! Some restraint has been practised however; we have not succumbed to the temptation of including 'fairy' cakes amongst the following recipes!

Melon and ham rolls
Small melon balls wrapped round with thin slices of sweet cured ham.

Celery bites
Small pieces of celery with a creamy cheese filling look lovely on the plate placed between the melon rolls.

Piquant cocktail sausages
Tiny chipolatas served warm with a lightly spiced dip – very more-ish.

Small mixed quiches
Little open pastry cases just 5cm (2in) across and filled with a delicious bacon or smooth cheese-based custard.

Spiral sandwiches
Made with an egg or salmon filling, these 'Swiss roll' type sandwiches look every bit as good as they taste.

Meringues with strawberry cream
Tiny white meringues sandwiched together with a strawberry cream are sure to delight anyone with a sweet tooth. Try serving them surrounded by spun sugar for a really magical touch.

Little fondant cakes
Covered in the prettiest shades of fondant icing, these small cakes are always popular.

Mini chocolate éclairs
One of the most favourite confections ever, these are made quite small to stay in keeping with the rest of the 'fairy' tea.

Fairy princess birthday cake
Using a Cindy doll and a 'crinoline' cake, this is one of the easiest and most popular birthday cakes for little girls. Try to design the 'dress' to match the season of the year; alternatively a bridal dress is one of the most popular designs.

The Drinks
Ice cream soda would be a most appropriate drink; the masses of froth look just 'right'! Put a small ball of vanilla ice cream into the bottom of a tall tumbler, pour over lemonade or cream soda, pop in a straw and a pretty cocktail decoration and serve. Have a few long-handled spoons ready so that any of the ice cream that doesn't melt can be eaten.

Recipes

MELON AND HAM ROLLS

1 melon (just ripe)
3–4 slices sweet-cured boiled ham
wooden cocktail sticks

To make
1) Halve the melon, scoop out and discard the seeds. Using a 'baller', cut out as many small balls of melon flesh as possible.
2) Trim any fat from the ham and cut the meat into strips about 2.5cm (1in) wide.
3) Roll a ham strip twice around each melon ball; secure each with a cocktail stick and chill.

CELERY BITES

100g (4oz) cream cheese
2 tablespoons double cream
salt and paprika pepper
1 tablespoon freshly chopped parsley (optional)
1 head of celery

To make
1) Mash the cheese and cream together with a fork until smooth
2) Season to taste and add the parsley if using.

3) Trim and wash the celery. Cut into pieces 3cm (1¼in)
   long. Fill with the cream cheese mixture. Sprinkle with
   a tiny amount of paprika pepper. Chill until needed.

PIQUANT COCKTAIL SAUSAGES

400g (1lb) cocktail chipolata sausages
wooden cocktail sticks
2 tablespoons mango chutney
2 tablespoons tomato ketchup
1 tablespoon brown sauce

To make
1) Preheat the grill. Separate the sausages and grill until
   golden brown on all sides. Spear with the cocktail
   sticks.
2) In a small bowl combine the chutney, ketchup and
   sauce, finely chopping any large pieces of mango.
3) Serve the sausages warm, arranged around the chutney
   dip.

SMALL MIXED QUICHES *(MAKES 24)*

For the shortcrust pastry

250g (10oz) plain flour
¼ teaspoon salt
125g (5oz) butter, chilled
cold water to mix

For the filling

2–3 tomatoes
2 large eggs

300ml (½pint) cream
300ml (½pint) milk
salt and freshly ground black pepper
2–3 rashers streaky bacon
1 small onion, chopped very finely
50g (2oz) Gruyère cheese, grated

To make

1) Sift the flour and salt into a large bowl. Cut the butter into small pieces and rub into the flour until the mixture resembles fine breadcrumbs. Mix to a firm dough with a little cold water. Chill for 30 minutes.
2) Dust a board with flour and roll out the pastry thinly. Cut into small rounds to fit your smallest patty tins – 6cm (2½in) diameter by 1cm (½in) deep would be ideal.
3) Line the patty tins with the pastry and chill again for 30 minutes. Preheat the oven to 220°C (425°F) Gas Mark 7.
4) Peel the tomatoes by covering with boiling water, waiting one minute then plunging into cold water. The skins will now come away easily. Slice into circles through the width of the tomato and push out and discard the seeds.
5) Beat the eggs thoroughly with the cream and milk, season with salt and a little pepper.
6) Derind the bacon and cut into tiny dice, fry in its own fat with the onion until brown and crisp.
7) Put a little bacon and onion mixture into half the patty tins and a small amount of grated cheese in the others. Cover the cheese with a tomato slice. Finally cover each quiche filling with the egg mixture.
8) Bake for 15–20 minutes until the pastry is cooked, the custard set and lightly browned. Serve warm or cold.

SPIRAL SANDWICHES

1 large uncut fine-textured loaf
1 large tin of salmon
2–3 drops lemon juice
150g (6oz) butter, softened

To Make
1) Trim the crusts from the bread and cut lengthways into thin slices, 8mm (⅓in) thick. Roll over each slice of bread with a rolling-pin and cover with a damp cloth to stop them drying out while you make the filling.
2) Drain the salmon, discarding any bones or skin, and mash to a paste with the lemon juice.
3) Spread the bread thickly with the butter then cover with the salmon paste. Roll up each slice of bread tightly, wrap with clingfilm and freeze for 1 hour.
4) Cut into rounds about 0.5cm (¼in) thick and serve.

MERINGUES WITH STRAWBERRY CREAM

For the meringue

4 egg whites
200g (8oz) caster sugar

1) Preheat the oven to 140°C (275°F) Gas Mark 1. Line a baking sheet with non-stick paper.
2) Whisk the egg whites until stiff, add the caster sugar a spoonful at a time, whisking well between each addition.
3) Pipe or spoon the mixture on to the prepared baking

sheet in tiny rounds about 3cm (1¼in) in diameter.
Bake for about 40–50 minutes until dry. Allow to cool.

For the strawberry cream

75g (3oz) butter, softened
150g (6oz) icing sugar
2 tablespoons strawberry jam

1) Cream the butter until light and fluffy. Gradually beat
   in the icing sugar.
2) Push the jam through a sieve and beat the resulting
   purée into the butter cream. Use to sandwich the
   meringues together.

For the spun sugar

400g (1lb) granulated sugar
300ml (½pint) water
good pinch of cream of tartar

you will also need a sugar thermometer

1) Bring the sugar and water to the boil in a saucepan.
   Boil until the syrup reaches 154°C (310°F). Stir in the
   cream of tartar and allow to cool.
2) When the syrup forms fine threads when dropped from
   a wooden spoon, it is ready for spinning.
3) Using a large metal spoon dipped first in oil then held
   horizontally and the wooden spoon, pass the syrup
   over the handle of the oiled spoon in loose circles,
   twirling the wooden spoon as you do so to give fine
   threads.
4) Place these fine threads around the outside of the plates
   and pile the little meringues into the centre.

LITTLE FONDANT CAKES *(Note: The fondant must be made 24 hours before using.)*

For the sponge cakes

125g (5oz) caster sugar
4 eggs
125g (5oz) plain flour
pinch of salt
50g (2oz) butter
3–4 tablespoons apricot glaze (see page 22)

1) Preheat the oven to 180°C (350°F) Gas Mark 4. Line a rectangular tin measuring 36 × 20 × 5cm (12 × 8 × 2in) with greaseproof paper.
2) Whisk the sugar and eggs together in a large bowl placed over a pan of hot water on a low heat. Continue to whisk until the batter is thick and white and leaves a trail when the whisk is lifted out. (It will take 10–20 minutes to reach this point, very boring but worth it!)
3) Sift the flour and salt on to a plate. Melt the butter and allow to cool.
4) Fold into the batter a third of the flour followed by a third of the butter, repeat twice. When the mixture is well blended, pour it into the prepared tin and bake for 20–25 minutes. Cool on a wire rack.

For the fondant

400g (1lb) granulated sugar
150ml (¼pint) water
2-3 drops food colourings

you will also need a sugar thermometer

1) Put the sugar and water into a pan and place over a medium heat. Stir gently until the sugar has completely dissolved.

2) Increase the heat and boil the syrup to the 'soft-ball' stage, 112–116°C (234–240°F). Stop the syrup cooking any further by placing the pan in cold water (careful, it splutters a little).
3) Pour a little water over a cold work surface. (Marble is best but a cold metal baking sheet will work well.) Pour the syrup on to the moist surface and allow to cool for 2–3 minutes.
4) Using a spatula or scraper dipped first in water, work the fondant over by lifting its edges over itself and folding into the centre. After about 10 minutes it will turn opaque then go very stiff.
5) Wet your hands then knead the fondant until smooth, 5–10 minutes. (Sorry it takes so long, the result *is* worth the effort, though).
6) Put the fondant into a bowl, cover with a damp cloth and leave for 24 hours in a cool place.

To finish the fondant cakes

1) Cut the sponge cake into small pieces; triangle and diamond shapes are best. Rounds and ovals also look very pretty and the left-over cake can be used as a trifle base. Whichever shapes you choose, try to keep them about 3cm (1¼in) across. Put on to a wire rack.
2) Warm the apricot glaze and liberally brush it on the top and sides of each little cake.
3) Place the bowl containing the fondant over a pan of hot water on a low heat. Melt the fondant in this way and then dilute it with a little water to the consistency of thick cream.
4) Separate the fondant into small warmed bowls, and add your chosen colourings, using only 1 or 2 drops of each so that the shades are very pale.
5) Pour the fondant over the cakes on the rack using the

edge of a knife to spread the icing over any missed areas.

6) When set, decorate either by piping thin lines of contrasting fondant over each cake, or with little pieces of cherry or flowers made from icing.

7) Put the fondant cakes into paper cases and keep cool.

MINI CHOCOLATE ÉCLAIRS

50g (2oz) butter
150ml (¼pint) water
50g (2oz) plain flour
2 eggs
large forcing bag and a plain round tube, 1cm (½in) diameter
150ml (¼pint) whipping cream
50g (2oz) dark chocolate

To make

1) Using a medium-sized pan melt the butter in the water and bring to the boil. Remove from the heat and tip in the flour. Beat well until the paste is smooth and forms a ball in the centre of the pan. Allow to cool for 1–2 minutes.

2) Whisk the eggs then beat them into the paste a little at a time until the mixture is well blended and glossy. Put into a large forcing bag and allow to 'rest' for 30 minutes. Preheat the oven to 200°C (400°F) Gas Mark 6.

3) Pipe small sausage-shapes, 4cm (1½in) long, on to a baking sheet. Bake for 30–35 minutes until well risen and light brown.

4) Cut each shape in half and put on a rack to cool.

5) Whip the cream and use to fill the centre of each éclair. Melt the chocolate with a little water and use to coat the top of each cake.

FAIRY PRINCESS BIRTHDAY CAKE

2 litre (2½pint) ovenproof pudding basin
200g (8oz) butter
200g (8oz) caster sugar
4 large eggs
200g (8oz) self-raising flour
2–3 drops vanilla essence
2 tablespoons hot water
1 Cindy doll (legs removed temporarily)
round cake board, silver or gold and measuring 25cm (10in) in diameter
3 tablespoons apricot glaze (see page 22)
satin icing made with 600g icing sugar (see page 22)
piping bags and tubes
ribbon for the 'waist'
a little royal icing (see page 23) for decorating the dress in different colours or all white if you are doing a bride cake
candles

To make

1) Preheat the oven to 180°C (350°F) Gas Mark 4. Grease the pudding basin.
2) Cream together the butter and sugar until light and very fluffy. Gradually beat in the eggs one at a time and when well blended sift in the flour. Fold this into the mixture using a metal spoon. Add the vanilla essence and hot water and turn into the pudding basin.

3) Bake the cake for 1 hour 15 minutes, allow to cool in the basin for 5 minutes then ease out gently and cool on a wire rack. (If by any chance you break the cake at this stage, don't worry about it. It can easily be sandwiched back into shape with a little apricot glaze).

4) Position the Cindy doll securely on top of the sponge cake and then place the cake in the centre of the board.

5) Brush the cake with warmed apricot glaze and then cover with the satin icing, smoothing down with your hands and arranging one or two 'gathers' in the skirt as you do so.

6) Using a piping bag with a small rose tube, pipe as ornate and pretty a decoration for the crinoline skirt as you can manage. Tie a pretty ribbon around the doll's waist, then pipe the top of the dress straight on to the doll's body.

7) Pipe large rosettes around the cake board and put in the candles just before they set.

6
Christmas Party
for ten to twenty 4–7 year olds

The Organization

First things first: someone *has* to be Father Christmas and the suit will need hiring in plenty of time so that there aren't any possible excuses on the day!

Invitations are easy: Christmas trees, Santas, stars, bells – there are so many traditional aspects of the Christmas festivities to choose from so just pick your children's favourites. However make sure that it is clear to your guests whether the party is to celebrate Christmas or a birthday, or both! Sometimes children with Christmas birthdays feel they 'miss out'!

Decorations shouldn't cause any problems at this party since all that's needed will probably be there already. It would be a nice touch to put up the tree and the lights just

before the party but, of course, this will depend on the date. Don't forget crackers for the table!

Games need to be all the old favourites – 'pass the parcel', 'musical chairs', etc, and there are always plenty of special Christmas records which are very appropriate for such games.

You will need to decide what sort of presents Santa is to dispense, bearing in mind that they all need to fit in his sack.

The Food

The choice of dishes for a Christmas party is all important; some traditional items will be expected but it is a good idea to steer well clear of anything remotely resembling a turkey dinner.

All the quantities in the recipes are for ten children – to cater for twenty, simply double up! Add crisps, a sausage hedgehog and small trifles to the following dishes to make an interesting Christmas party 'spread'.

Small chicken goujons with a choice of dips
Crisp coated pieces of chicken breast served warm with one hot and one cold dip.

Cheese and ham roll-ups
An ingenious way of baking cheese and ham sandwiches.

Tea bread
A moist and delicious malted loaf – lovely with a little butter.

Small chocolate logs
Miniature versions of the traditional chocolate yule log. Always a great favourite.

Meringue snowmen
Easy-to-make little snowmen of melt-in-the-mouth meringue with a cream filling, decorated with chocolate buttons.

Santa's sleigh cake
A special party cake or even a birthday cake if the party is
to celebrate a Christmas birthday. Gingerbread reindeer
pull a soft sponge sleigh absolutely loaded with tiny gifts.
Great fun!

The Drinks
The usual favourites, orange juice, lemonade etc, will be
fine for the children but do try to have a warm drink
ready for collecting parents – it will be much appreciated
especially if the weather is seasonal.

Recipes

SMALL CHICKEN GOUJONS WITH TWO DIPS

4 chicken breasts, skinned and boned
4 tablespoons flour
salt and freshly ground black pepper
1 egg, beaten with 1 tablespoon milk
4 tablespoons fresh brown breadcrumbs
25g (1oz) butter
4 tablespoons olive oil
wooden cocktail sticks

To make

1) Cut each chicken breast into six strips. Mix the flour with some salt and pepper and toss the chicken pieces in it.
2) Shake the excess flour from the chicken strips then dip them into the egg wash, a few at a time.
3) Roll the chicken strips in the breadcrumbs and then chill for 30 minutes.
4) Heat the butter and oil in a frying pan. When the foam subsides cook the goujons (in two batches) for about 3 minutes each side or until golden brown. Drain on kitchen paper.
5) Arrange the goujons on a warmed plate, insert a cocktail stick in each one and serve with one hot and one cold dip.

Hot dip

25g (1oz) butter
1 tablespoon oil
1 medium onion, finely chopped
1 large tin of tomatoes, drained and chopped
1 tablespoon Worcestershire sauce
salt and cayenne pepper

1) Heat the butter and oil in a small pan. Cook the onion slowly until soft and well browned.
2) Add the other ingredients and season very lightly with salt and cayenne pepper. Cook on a low heat for 10–15 minutes until fairly thick. Check the seasoning and serve.

Cold dip

4 tablespoons natural yoghurt
½ teaspoon concentrated mint sauce
salt and freshly ground black pepper

1) Beat the yoghurt with a whisk until light. Mix in the mint sauce, season to taste and serve.

CHEESE AND HAM ROLL-UPS

1 white sandwich loaf, uncut and 1 day old
150g (6oz) soft butter
200g (8oz) Cheddar cheese, grated
200g (8oz) boiled ham, thinly sliced
2 tablespoons melted butter

To make

1) Preheat the oven to 230°C (450°F) Gas Mark 8.
2) Trim the crusts from the bread and cut thinly into slices.

3) Spread each slice of bread thickly with butter and cover half of it with a slice of ham. Sprinkle over some grated cheese and roll up into a sausage shape. Chill for 30 minutes.

4) Brush the rolls with melted butter and bake for 6–8 minutes until crisp and light brown.

N.B. The rolls can be made up the day before the party, wrapped in clingfilm, then cooked as needed. Other fillings are cheese and grated onion, cheese and prawn, or cheese and fresh mixed herbs.

TEA BREAD

300g (12oz) self-raising flour
½ teaspoon salt
25g (1oz) butter
50g (2oz) soft brown sugar
100g (4oz) sultanas
50g (2oz) chopped walnuts
50g (2oz) cherries, chopped small
150ml (¼ pint) milk
50g (2oz) black treacle
50g (2oz) malt extract
2 eggs

To make

1) Preheat the oven to 180°C (350°F) Gas Mark 4. Grease and line a 23 × 12cm (9 × 5in) loaf tin.

2) Sift the flour and salt into a mixing bowl. Add the butter and rub into the flour, using your fingertips.

3) Mix in the sugar and fruit.

4) Warm the milk, treacle and malt extract in a pan and stir well. Beat the eggs and mix in.

5) Pour the treacle mixture over the flour mixture and beat until well combined. Turn the mixture into the loaf tin and bake for about 1 hour. Allow the loaf to cool in the tin then turn out on to a wire rack.
6) Serve sliced and spread with butter.

SMALL CHOCOLATE LOGS

3 eggs
100g (4oz) caster sugar
100g (4oz) plain flour mixed with 1 tablespoon cocoa
   powder
1 tablespoon hot water
4 tablespoons raspberry jam, warmed

To make
1) Preheat the oven to 220°C (425°F) Gas Mark 7. Grease ar.d line two 30 × 23cm (12 × 9in) Swiss roll tins.
2) Beat the eggs and sugar together in a large bowl set over a pan of hot water until the mixture is so thick that the whisk leaves a trail when removed. Take the bowl from the heat and sift in the flour mixture.
3) Fold in the flour with a metal spoon and then fold in the hot water gently. Divide the mixture between the two prepared tins. Bake for 6–8 minutes.
4) Wring out two clean tea towels in water and place side by side on a work surface. Cover with greaseproof paper.
5) Turn the cakes out, straight on to the damp paper; trim the edges and spread the cakes with the warmed jam.
6) Roll up each cake *lengthways*, using the paper to help obtain a good shape.

Chocolate butter icing

  100g (4oz) butter
  200g (8oz) icing sugar
  2 tablespoons cocoa powder
  2 tablespoons hot water
  1 tablespoon milk

1) Beat the butter and half the icing sugar together in a
   bowl until smooth.
2) Mix the cocoa and hot water together; blend well then
   add the milk.
3) When cool beat the cocoa mixture into the butter
   mixture along with the remaining icing sugar.

Cream butter icing

  50g (2oz) butter
  100g (4oz) icing sugar
  1 tablespoon milk

1) Beat the butter and half the icing sugar together in a
   bowl until smooth.
2) Slowly add the milk and the rest of the icing sugar and
   blend well.

To finish the logs

  chocolate butter icing
  cream butter icing
  piping bags and a small rosette tube
  small robins or holly sprigs

1) Cut the rolls into short lengths, about 8cm (3in) long.
   Cover the tops and sides with the chocolate icing and
   the ends with the cream icing. (This looks most effective when piped in a spiral on the ends to resemble the

log's rings and in wavy lines along the top and sides to resemble bark.
2) Place the robins or holly sprigs on top of the rolls and chill.

MERINGUE SNOWMEN

2 egg whites
100g (4oz) caster sugar
small bag of milk chocolate buttons
150ml (¼ pint) double cream
red wool or ribbon for scarves

To make

1) Preheat the oven to 150°C (300°F) Gas Mark 2. Line a baking sheet with non-stick silicone paper.
2) Whisk the egg whites until stiff then whisk in half the sugar, a tablespoon at a time, until the mixture is very stiff and glossy. Fold in the remaining sugar with a metal spoon.
3) Either pipe or spoon the mixture on to the baking sheet to form small rounds for the heads and larger rounds for the bodies. (They look more authentic when a little uneven.)
4) Put the baking sheet into the oven and immediately turn the heat down to 110°C (200°F) Gas Mark ¼. Leave for 2 hours. Remove the tray from the oven and gently lift each meringue and turn it on to its side. Turn the oven off but leave the meringues inside it for a further hour.
5) To assemble the snowmen, whip the cream and use to attach the heads to the bodies. Tie a 'scarf' around each neck and cut up the chocolate buttons into small pieces

to use for the facial features and the coat buttons.
Reserve several whole chocolate buttons to use as
'hats'. Stick them on to the meringue snowmen with a
little jam or cream.

SANTA'S SLEIGH CAKE

For the cake

200g (8oz) butter
200g (8oz) caster sugar
4 eggs
200g (8oz) self-raising flour
2 tablespoons hot water

1) Preheat the oven to 180°C (350°F) Gas Mark 4. Grease
   and line a 23 × 12cm (9 × 5in) loaf tin.
2) Cream the butter and sugar together until light and
   fluffy. Beat in the eggs. Sift in the flour and fold this
   into the mixture with a metal spoon. Stir in the water
   gently.
3) Turn the mixture into the baking tin and cook for
   1½–1¾ hours.

For the gingerbread reindeer

200g (8oz) plain flour
½ teaspoon bicarbonate of soda
1 teaspoon ground ginger
75g (3oz) butter
100g (4oz) soft brown sugar
1 egg
2 tablespoons golden syrup

1) Preheat the oven to 190°C (375°F) Gas Mark 5. Grease a large baking tray.
2) Sift the flour, bicarbonate of soda and ginger into a bowl and rub in the butter and sugar.
3) Beat the egg, syrup and sugar together and when mixed pour into the bowl over the flour. Gather together and knead until smooth.
4) Flour a board lightly, then roll out the gingerbread to 1cm (⅜in) thick. In the absence of reindeer cutters use 10cm (4in) horse or donkey cutters. Carefully transfer the animal shapes to the baking sheet.
5) Bake for about 15 minutes, until golden brown. Cool on a wire rack.

To finish the cake

    large long board measuring about 50 × 20cm (20 × 8in) or use a much smaller board just under the sleigh
    3–4 tablespoons apricot glaze (see page 22)
    red satin icing made with 600g (1½lb) icing sugar (see page 22)
    6–8 tablespoons white royal icing (see page 23)
    piping bags and a No 2 writing tube
    thin cord or gift-wrap string to use as reins
    several new white pipe cleaners
    1 red Smartie for Rudolf's nose
    50g (2oz) almond paste
    candles and holders (optional)

1) Cut the cake into a thick wedge shape curving the back slightly. Cut out the centre of the sleigh to make room for the presents (the 'cut-offs' can be used as trifle bases).
2) Put the sleigh on to the cake board, warm the apricot glaze and brush it all over the cake inside and out.

3) Cover the cake with the satin icing, moulding it with your hands to give a smooth finish.

4) Pipe a panel design on to the sides of the sleigh with some of the white royal icing.

5) Pipe faces and harnesses on to the reindeer, attaching the reins as you do so. Twist the pipe cleaners to form antlers and attach these to the heads. Stand the reindeer two by two in front of the sleigh, secured with a little almond paste.

6) Roll the remaining almond paste into long thin sausage shapes with a swirl at one end. Press along the bottom of the sleigh to form the runners.

7) Stick on a red Smartie for Rudolf's nose and position the candles, if using. Put the presents gently into the back of the sleigh.

7
Bar-b-que party
for ten 6+ year olds

The Organization

Bar-b-ques are extremely popular with all children; the food combines most of their favourite things and there's no hassle about exemplary table manners! Some provision will need to be made in case the weather is awful but that apart, the atmosphere for a bar-b-que should be as free and easy as possible.

'Dead lions' is a fun game for this sort of gathering as are many of the 'running about' games that are best played out of doors. If your lawn is fairly big, try a five-a-side football match or put a volley ball net across it and play for reduced time periods.

Remember to light the bar-b-que about 1 hour before you want to start to cook. A trestle table covered with a bright paper tablecloth will be invaluable for putting all the bits and pieces on. Paper plates can be a good idea but

you need the stronger variety that are suitable for hot food. Lots of paper napkins and some moist tissues are essential. Put the plates and napkins on the trestle table along with any ketchups or relishes you need.

Try to position the table between the bar-b-que and yourself, away from where the children will be standing. Perhaps an 'L' shape would work best and the food could be put straight on to the table then the guests can help themselves to salad and potatoes leaving you free to supervise the bar-b-que at all times.

If you are combining a disco with the bar-b-que allow for a party lasting up to three hours, otherwise stick to the popular two-hour period.

The Food

Hamburgers
Even bought burgers taste better bar-b-qued. It is simple to make your own but if time is short buy the best quality made-up burgers you can find.

Hot dogs
Very good made with a decent sausage instead of frankfurters, which can be a little insipid. Try a bar-b-que sauce with them, instead of mustard.

Devilled chicken legs
These chicken legs are partially cooked before being bar-b-qued which solves the problem of making sure they're cooked through to the centre without the outside resembling charcoal.

Corn on the cob
Fresh corn in its husk is a good vegetable to bar-b-que and delicious with melted butter.

Criss-cross potatoes
Slices of potato cooked on the bar-b-que make a change from potatoes in jackets and have a marvellous flavour.

Bananas cooked in their skins
'Carry-on bar-b-queing!' Even the sweets are cooked over charcoal at this party!

Fruit kebabs
Pineapple, peaches, apples, pears, apricots and plums are all most suitable to make these delicious kebabs.

In addition to the above dishes make up a large combination salad. (Remember most children love salad cream so have some on hand.) Don't forget to put out some crisps.

Football birthday cake
A popular cake for boys, it is easy to make and looks good when served outside. (Some cakes look silly in bright sunlight!)

The Drinks
Something long, fruity and cooling is best for bar-b-ques. Try blending pineapple and orange juice with crushed apricots and serving poured over crushed ice. Alternatively, try a punch.

Mayflower punch

   400g (1lb) sugar
   1.2 litres (2pints) water
   800g (2lb) strawberries, puréed
   juice of 4 oranges
   juice of 2 lemons
   1 whole fresh pineapple, peeled and grated
   300ml (½pint) tea
   800g (2lb) crushed ice
   1.2 litres (2pints) soda water

1) Heat the sugar and 300ml (½pint) water in a large saucepan. Bring to the boil and simmer for 5 minutes.

2) Put in the strawberry purée, fruit juices, grated pine-apple and tea. Leave to cool.

3) Put the crushed ice into a punch bowl, pour over the punch, then add the soda water and the remaining water. Serve at once.

Recipes

HAMBURGERS

1kg (2lb) lean topside of beef
50g (2oz) butter, softened
salt and freshly ground black pepper

To make
1) Trim the meat of all fat and gristle. Cut into strips and put through a mincer using a medium blade.
2) Mix in the butter and season well. Form into small patties by rolling into balls with your hands, then flattening out to a thickness of about 1cm (½in). Chill until needed.
3) Bar-b-que for about 5 minutes each side.

To serve
Soft buns with sesame seeds on top are the traditional container for a hamburger. Have salads, relishes and a bar-b-que sauce (see following recipe) on hand for your guests to help themselves.

BAR-B-QUE SAUCE

600g (1½lb) ripe tomatoes
1 tablespoon olive oil
1 onion, finely chopped
½ teaspoon dried thyme

50g (2oz) brown sugar
2 tablespoons vinegar
1 tablespoon Worcestershire sauce
salt and pepper

To make

1) Peel the tomatoes by covering with boiling water, leaving for 1 minute then plunging into cold water after which the skins will come away easily. Chop roughly.
2) Heat the oil in a saucepan, put in the onion and cook until soft but not brown. Put in the tomatoes and thyme and continue cooking until the tomatoes become a pulp.
3) Add the sugar, vinegar and Worcestershire sauce together with ¼ teaspoon of salt and a little pepper.
4) Simmer gently for about 10 minutes. Check seasoning.

HOT DOGS

50g (2oz) butter
2 large onions, thinly sliced into rings
400g (1 lb) good pork sausages
soft finger rolls

To make

1) Melt the butter in a frying pan, add the onions and cook until soft and very brown. Keep warm.
2) Grill the sausages on the bar-b-que for 10–15 minutes until cooked through and browned.
3) Split the rolls in half along one side. Put in a sausage and some onions. Serve with bar-b-que sauce and mustard.

DEVILLED CHICKEN LEGS

12–14 chicken drumsticks
1 small onion
1 small carrot
1 stick of celery
salt and freshly ground black pepper
200g (8oz) softened butter
2 tablespoons Worcestershire sauce
4 tablespoons tomato ketchup
4 tablespoons mango chutney

To make
1) Put the chicken legs into a large pan with the onion peeled and cut into two, the carrot peeled and chopped in chunks, and the celery chopped into large pieces. Season lightly, cover with water and bring to the boil.
2) Turn the heat to medium and simmer for 15 minutes. Allow to cool. Drain well.
3) Cream the butter and beat in the Worcestershire sauce, ketchup and chutney, season lightly.
4) Skin the chicken legs and spread with the devilled mixture. Chill for at least 2 hours.
5) Bar-b-que the drumsticks for about 6 minutes per side, basting with any left-over devilled sauce as they cook. (Although these chicken legs are to be served hot on this occasion, they are equally delicious when cold, but rather sticky!)

CORN ON THE COB

8–12 ears of sweetcorn
string for tying
butter to serve

To cook

1) Pull the green leaves back from the corn very gently (they need to stay attached). Pull out and discard the fine threads that surround the corn. Wrap the leaves back into position and tie at the top or secure with string.

2) Cook on the bar-b-que, turning frequently, for about 15 minutes or until the husks are dark brown on all sides.

3) Remove the string, open the husks and put butter on to the kernels before serving.

CRISS-CROSS POTATOES

4–5 large potatoes
2 tablespoons olive oil
salt and freshly ground black pepper

To make

1) Scrub the potatoes well and boil whole in their skins until almost cooked. Drain well and cool.

2) Pour the oil on to a shallow plate, season. Cut the potatoes lengthways into 8mm (⅓in) slices. Put each slice into the oil and coat on both sides.

3) Grill the potato slices on the bar-b-que for 3 minutes, then turn through 90° (hence the criss-cross) Turn over and repeat the process on the underside. Serve at once.

BANANAS COOKED IN THEIR SKINS

8–12 bananas (not over-ripe)
100g (4oz) caster sugar
whipped cream

To make

1) Lay each banana on a work surface and, using a small sharp knife, cut the top part of the skin from the banana, leave the underside intact. Sprinkle with sugar.
2) Grill on the bar-b-que, skin side down, for about 5 minutes until the sugar has melted. Serve with whipped cream.

N.B. These bananas are marvellous flambéed. Pour a little warmed kirsch over each one and set alight just before serving. (Do this well away from the bar-b-que.) Again serve with whipped cream.

FRUIT KEBABS

800g (2lb) mixed fruit – choose from apples, pears, peaches, nectarines, plums, pineapples, oranges and bananas
juice of 2 lemons
skewers
50g (2oz) sugar

To make

1) Cut the fruit into pieces about 3cm (1in) square. Brush the pieces with lemon juice to prevent discoloration. Thread on to skewers.
2) Cook over the bar-b-que, turning frequently, for 5–10 minutes. Sprinkle with sugar and let it darken slightly. Serve at once.

FOOTBALL BIRTHDAY CAKE

2 × 900ml (1½pint) ovenproof pudding basins
200g (8oz) butter
200g (8oz) caster sugar
4 eggs, beaten
200g (8oz) self-raising flour
2 tablespoons hot water

To make

1) Preheat the oven to 180°C (350°F) Gas Mark 4. Grease and flour the pudding basins.
2) Cream the butter and sugar together until light and fluffy. Beat in the egg mixture a little at a time; sift in the flour and fold into the mixture with a metal spoon. Fold in the hot water.
3) Divide the mixture between the two basins and bake for 1¼–1½ hours. Turn out on to a wire rack to cool.

Chocolate butter icing

2 tablespoons cocoa powder
2 tablespoons hot water
200g (8oz) butter
400g (1lb) icing sugar
1 tablespoon milk

1) Mix the cocoa powder and hot water together to a smooth paste.
2) Cream the butter and 100g (4oz) of icing sugar until light and fluffy.
3) Add the cocoa paste, milk and remaining icing sugar and beat well until light and creamy. Store in an airtight container for up to 4 weeks in the fridge.

To finish the cake

1 large cake board 30cm (12in) square
green-coloured butter cream made with 50g (2oz) butter
    (see page 20)
3–4 tablespoons green-coloured coconut
2 tablespoons apricot glaze (see page 22)
chocolate butter icing
piping bags and a No 2 writing tube
small amount of white royal icing (see page 23)
candles

1) Cover the cake board with the green butter cream. Sprinkle with the coconut to look like turf.
2) Trim the cakes to form a good round shape leaving the underside flat so that it sits properly on the cake board.
3) Sandwich the two halves together with a little warmed apricot glaze and position on the cake board.
4) Spread the chocolate butter icing over the cake as smoothly as possible.
5) Mark the 'seaming' on the football using a crinkly-edged pastry wheel. Allow the icing to set.
6) Pipe the child's name on to the cake using the white icing and go around the seams with tiny white dots for the stitching. Make thicker lines for the lacings and any relevant numbers you wish to include.
7) Position the candles on the cake board with the aid of some butter cream.

8
Magic Party
for twelve 7–9 year olds

The Organization

Although this party has magic as its theme and it would be rather special to invite a magician to entertain the children, this is by no means essential. There are so many magic kits and tricks available that all you'll need to do it yourself is announce 'IZZY WHIZZY, LET'S GET BUSY!' You might even get some help with the tidying up!

The simplest invitation card to make would be a conical hat shape, just like the one Merlin wears. Put a few strands of wool at the top and a couple of silver stick-on-stars and moons near the bottom edge, then write the wording in the middle with a fluorescent pen. The pen can also be used most effectively on name cards while the stick-on-stars and moons make good prize tokens.

Old playing cards strung together make a good decoration, especially when secured around the tablecloth. Top hats cut from cardboard with pop-up rabbits are fun when positioned around the room.

As guests are arriving it would be fun to invite them to look around for riddles and small puzzles which you have previously left about, correct solutions earning silver stars as prizes. Do try to give a magical touch to all the games you have planned – even 'pinning the wand in the magician's hand' would be better than nothing.

If you *are* having a magic show you won't need quite so many games; two hours is still the most workable duration for most children's parties and the best time to have the magic show is straight after the food when the children are more likely to be in the mood for sitting still. Make sure everyone has a good view otherwise they will fidget!

The Food

Older children will be able to cope with the Danish-style open sandwiches that are served as the main course of this party. Two sausage and cheese hedgehogs (see page 45) should be made in addition to the items below and of course the ever-popular crisps should also be put out.

Danish open sandwiches
A great way to use lots of different fillings; these sandwiches look most attractive. Serve with a fish slice and make sure the children have knives and forks in order to tackle them properly.

Potato salad with hot bacon dressing
Served warm this salad is an excellent accompaniment to the open sandwiches and just a little bit different.

Vanilla fortune cookies
Great fun to make; leave yourself time to devise some hilarious fortunes!

Little iced fancies
Small cup cakes iced with cryptic messages – remember Alice and the 'eat me' cake?

Top hat and rabbits birthday cake
A soft sponge cake hat and crunchy biscuit rabbits make an interesting birthday cake, perfect for a magic party.

The Drinks

Try a frothy milk-shake served with straws in tall glasses.
Orange is a most unusual and refreshing flavour.

600ml (1pint) milk
2 tablespoons double cream
juice of 3 oranges mixed with the juice of half a lemon
4 tablespoons caster sugar

Put everything into a blender, switch on for 2 minutes or
so. Pour the mixture over ice cubes in tall sundae glasses.
Put in two straws and dangle a twist of orange peel over
the rim.

Recipes

DANISH OPEN SANDWICHES

Children prefer a white bread base to the more usual rye or pumpernickel, but whichever bread you choose it needs to be quite thickly cut – about 8mm (⅓in) – and trimmed of crusts. Spread each slice of bread liberally with softened butter, allowing 2 slices per person. Cover with a selection of fillings from the list below or concoct your own. (Try to keep a small amount of each filling on one side, there is always one child who must have exactly the same as his/her friend!)

Boiled ham with gherkin fans and sliced tomato
Trim away any fat from the ham first.

Liver sausage with beetroot
Choose a mild liver sausage; the very garlicky ones are not suitable and make everything around them smell too – most off-putting – especially for children.

Hard-boiled eggs sliced and topped with a few prawns and a tomato mayonnaise
Garnish with a twist of cucumber or a pinch of lump fish 'caviar'. (Make the mayonnaise by adding 1 teaspoon tomato ketchup to 1 tablespoon mayonnaise.)

Sardines on soft scrambled eggs with slices of tomato

*Cold roast pork with mango chutney and little sage-
and-onion-stuffing balls*

Cottage cheese with pineapple and prawns

*Crisp grilled bacon (cold) with lettuce, tomato slices
and mayonnaise*

*Cold roast chicken with seedless grapes and sliced
radishes*

POTATO SALAD WITH HOT BACON DRESSING

800g (2lb) potatoes
4 rashers lean bacon, derinded and chopped
1 medium onion, finely chopped
salt and freshly ground black pepper
1 tablespoon wine vinegar
3 tablespoons olive oil

To make
1) Boil the potatoes in their skins until cooked. Keep
   warm.
2) Using a small pan fry the bacon pieces in their own fat
   with the onion until both are lightly browned.
3) Mix some salt and pepper with the vinegar and stir to
   dissolve the salt. Beat in the olive oil. Add the mixture
   to the bacon and onions, bring to the boil then reduce
   the heat and simmer for 1–2 minutes.
4) Peel the hot potatoes and cut them either into slices or
   chunks. Pour over the dressing and serve.

VANILLA FORTUNE COOKIES

150g (6oz) butter
100g (4oz) caster sugar
2 small egg yolks
2–3 drops vanilla essence
175g (7oz) self-raising flour

fortunes typed or written on small pieces of white
   cartridge paper folded into four

To make
1) Preheat the oven to 190°C (375°F) Gas Mark 5. Grease
   two large baking sheets.
2) Cream the butter and sugar together until light and
   fluffy. Beat in the egg yolks and vanilla essence. Fold
   in the flour.
3) Gather into a stiff dough and shape into small balls,
   putting a 'fortune' into the centre of each one.
4) Put the cookies on to the baking sheets and cook for
   15–20 minutes. Leave to cool for a few minutes on the
   trays then gently lift on to a wire rack.

Warning
Do make sure that all the children know about the paper
fortunes. It isn't easy to eat cartridge paper, but there's
always an exception!

LITTLE ICED FANCIES

100g (4oz) butter
100g (4oz) caster sugar
2 eggs, beaten
100g (4oz) self-raising flour, sifted

16–20 small paper cases
100g (4oz) icing sugar
1–2 drops food colouring (optional)
edible food colouring pens *or* melted chocolate

To make

1) Preheat the oven to 190°C (375°F) Gas Mark 5. Put the paper cases on to baking sheets.
2) Cream the butter and sugar until light and fluffy. Beat in the egg mixture a little at a time, then fold in the flour using a metal spoon.
3) Spoon the mixture into the paper cases and bake for 15–20 minutes until golden brown. Cool on a wire rack.
4) Make up the icing by adding 2–3 drops of water to the icing sugar. Stir until smooth, adding a little food colouring if wished. Pour the icing on top of each little cake (the paper cases will keep it in place). Allow to set.
5) Write names or messages on the cakes using the special food colouring pens or melted chocolate.

TOP HAT AND RABBITS BIRTHDAY CAKE

For the sponge cake

3 deep round cake tins, 15cm (6in) diameter (or make in three lots)
300g (12oz) butter
300g (12oz) caster sugar
6 eggs, beaten
300g (12oz) self-raising flour
25g (1oz) cocoa

3 tablespoons hot water
2–3 drops food colouring (strawberry red)

To make
1) Preheat the oven to 180°C (350°F) Gas Mark 4. Grease and line the cake tins.
2) Cream the butter and sugar together until light and fluffy. Beat in the egg mixture a little at a time; fold in the flour using a metal spoon.
3) Divide the mixture into three. Fold the cocoa into one mix, 2–3 drops strawberry food colouring into another, and leave the third plain. Turn the mixtures into the prepared tins and bake for 1¼–1½ hours. Turn on to a wire rack to cool.

For the shortbread rabbits
150g (6oz) plain flour
50g (2oz) caster sugar
100g (4oz) butter
rabbit-shaped cutters or use a gingerbread-man shape
   (see method, stage 3)

1) Preheat the oven to 170°C (375°F) Gas Mark 3. Grease a large baking sheet.
2) Mix together the flour and sugar. Put in the butter in one piece and mix into the flour and sugar with your fingers.
3) Knead well then pat or roll out as thinly as possible. Cut into rabbit shapes and put on the prepared baking sheet.
   To cut out with a gingerbread-man shape, put the shape on to the shortbread and press gently just so that you have a line to cut round. Use a sharp knife and give the rabbit free-hand ears – one could even be

bent! Lift the shapes on to the baking sheet gently using a fish slice.

4) Bake for 40 minutes until golden brown. Cool on a wire rack.

To finish the cake

vanilla butter cream made with 50g (2oz) butter (see page 20)

silver cake board, 30cm (12in) square

3–4 tablespoons apricot glaze (see page 22)

piece of cardboard 23cm (9in) in diameter to form the brim of the 'hat'

black butter cream made with 300g (12oz) butter (see page 20)

piping bags, a small rose tube and a No 2 writing tube

white ribbon to go round the 'hat'

a small amount of royal icing (see page 23) for eyes and whiskers on the rabbits

candles and holders

one or two sticks of liquorice for the 'wands'

1) Level the sponge cakes and sandwich together with some of the vanilla butter cream. Arrange them with the chocolate cake at the top, then the strawberry cake, and the plain cake at the bottom.

2) Place the assembled cake on the board and cut out a centre piece about 10cm (4in) in diameter and 10cm (4in) deep (the cut-out pieces of cake can be used as trifle bases). Brush the cake surface with apricot glaze.

3) Position the cardboard brim on top of the cake making sure the centre hole coincides with the hole in the cake.

4) Cover the cake and the brim with black butter cream (black edible food colouring is available but if preferred use a dark chocolate frosting). Put some vanilla butter

cream into a piping bag loaded with a small rose tube. Pipe small rosettes around the edges of the hat and brim.

5) Secure the ribbon round the cake just below the brim.
6) Using the royal icing pipe eyes and whiskers on the shortbread rabbits. Use a small blob of the icing to secure the liquorice wands in one or two of the rabbits' hands. When dry, arrange them in the centre of the hat.
7) Pipe rosettes on to the hat's brim to hold the candles.

9
Hallowe'en Party
for ten children 7+ years old

The Organization

Hallowe'en seems to have a special appeal for children and many parents are deciding to make more of this date than the Guy Fawkes night that follows it so closely.

Invitations can be in the form of witches' hats, spiders' webs, pumpkins or cauldrons. The decor must be dark and gloomy, but if there are to be very young children present don't overdo this! Fluorescent pens are super to use for the decorations and black cotton is useful for creating spiders' webs or tying little witches on broomsticks to drawing pins in the ceiling.

It really is worth taking the time to hollow out a pumpkin face for the centre of the table; turnip faces placed around the room are also most effective. (We give

recipes for American pumpkin pie and turnip soup so neither decoration is wasteful). Be careful where you site the turnips though, because of the candles inside.

Fancy dress is a popular choice for Hallowe'en and most children really enjoy this aspect of the celebrations. By far the easiest and most suitable costume is an old white sheet with holes cut out for the eyes.

Certain games are traditional to Hallowe'en, like 'bobbing for apples', but almost any other favourite game could be adopted to fit in with the party's theme.

The Food

Turnip soup
A very satisfying soup to make, it takes no time at all and the results are delicious.

Pork chops with spicy tomato sauce
Pork chops cooked in a 'yummy' sauce until very tender. Not too sophisticated for youngsters.

Cheesy jacket potatoes
Baked potatoes with the centres mashed with cheese then grilled.

American pumpkin pie
What else? This recipe is really an open flan but still quite traditional. Good served with ice-cream.

Crunchy apple crumble
An alternative to the pumpkin pie; the topping uses muesli to give it the crunch.

Spider cakes
Little sponge cakes with chocolate match-stick legs – ugh, but they taste great!

The Drinks
A warmed fruit punch is ideal; try chopping an apple, banana and pear into blackcurrant cordial and heat gently.

Recipes

TURNIP SOUP

400g (1lb) turnip flesh, chopped
300g (12oz) potatoes
1 medium onion
1 leek
50g (2oz) butter
25g (1oz) flour
2.5 litres (4pints) chicken stock
salt and freshly ground black pepper
3 large egg yolks
3 tablespoons double cream
croutons to garnish

To make
1) Peel and dice the potatoes and mix with the turnip.
2) Peel and slice the onion and leek. Melt the butter in a large saucepan. Cook the onion and leek until soft but not brown. Sprinkle on the flour and stir to mix in. Put the potatoes and turnips into the pan and cover with the stock. Season well.
3) Bring to the boil then turn the heat to low and simmer for 30–40 minutes or until the vegetables are cooked.
4) Pour the soup into a liquidizer and blend, or push through a sieve. Re-heat when needed.
5) To finish the soup, first beat the egg yolks and cream together in a small basin. Beat in 2 tablespoons of the hot soup then stir all the egg mixture into the soup

where it will thicken. Stir over a low heat for 2–3 minutes. Serve with bread croutons.

PORK CHOPS WITH SPICY TOMATO SAUCE

10 small pork loin chops
salt and freshly ground black pepper
1 large onion
1 clove garlic
3 tablespoons vegetable oil
1 large tin tomatoes
1 tablespoon tomatoe purée
2 tablespoons wine vinegar
3 tablespoons Worcestershire sauce
4 tablespoons honey
¼ teaspoon chilli powder
¼ teaspoon mustard powder
½ teaspoon salt

To make
1) Preheat the oven to 190°C (375°F) Gas Mark 5. Sprinkle the chops with salt and pepper and bake for 20 minutes.
2) While the chops are baking, make the sauce. First peel and thinly slice the onion and chop the garlic.
3) Heat the oil and fry the onion and garlic until soft and golden brown.
4) Add all the other sauce ingredients and simmer for 10 minutes.
5) Pour the sauce over the partly cooked chops and bake for a further 20–30 minutes or until the meat is tender.

CHEESY JACKET POTATOES

5 very large potatoes or 10 medium-sized ones
1 egg yolk
50g (2oz) butter
50g (2oz) Cheddar cheese, grated
salt and freshly ground black pepper
tomato slices
parsley to garnish

To make
1) Preheat the oven to 180°C (350°F) Gas Mark 4. Scrub the potatoes well and score a line lengthways around the centre of each one. Bake for 1–1½ hours or until soft.
2) Cut each potato in half using the scored line as a guide. Carefully scoop out the potato using a small spoon.
3) Mash the potato with the egg yolk, butter and cheese. Pile the mixture back into the potato shells, pop a tomato slice on top and grill until lightly browned. Garnish with a sprig of parsley.

AMERICAN PUMPKIN PIE

200g (8oz) shortcrust pastry (see method, page 79)
400g (1lb) pumpkin flesh
3 eggs
150ml (¼pint) double cream
150ml (¼pint) milk
300g (6oz) soft dark brown sugar
½ teaspoon cinnamon
pinch of ground cloves
¼ teaspoon ground ginger

To make

1) Preheat the oven to 180°C (350°F) Gas Mark 4.
2) Roll out the pastry and use to line a 23cm (9in) flan dish. Chill for 30 minutes.
3) Cut up the pumpkin flesh and cook gently until soft. Drain and push through a sieve to give 200g (8oz) purée.
4) Beat the eggs and mix with the cream, milk, sugar, spices and pumpkin purée.
5) Pour the mixture into the flan dish and bake for 40–45 minutes until well set.
6) Serve just warm with whipped cream or ice-cream.

CRUNCHY APPLE CRUMBLE

800g (2lb) cooking apples, Bramleys for preference
50g (2oz) soft brown sugar
2 tablespoons water
100g (4oz) self-raising flour
75g (3oz) butter, softened
100g (4oz) muesli
100g (4oz) soft brown sugar

To make

1) Preheat the oven to 180°C (350°F) Gas Mark 4.
2) Peel and slice the apples and put into the bottom of a deep dish. Sprinkle with the 50g (2oz) soft brown sugar and the 2 tablespoons water.
3) Sift the flour into a bowl and rub in the butter until the mixture resembles fine breadcrumbs. Mix in the muesli and the 100g (4oz) sugar and pile the mixture on top of the apples. Bake for 30–40 minutes.
4) Serve warm with ice-cream.

SPIDER CAKES

50g (2oz) butter
50g (2oz) caster sugar
1 egg
50g (2oz) self-raising flour
½ tablespoon hot water
2 tablespoons apricot glaze (see page 22)
4 tablespoons white royal icing (see page 23)
chocolate matchsticks

To make

1) Preheat the oven to 180°C (350°F) Gas Mark 4. Grease a bun tin (for small buns).
2) Cream the butter and sugar together until light and fluffy. Beat in the egg and then sift in the flour. Fold the flour into the mixture using a metal spoon. Gently stir in the water. Turn the mixture into the bun tin and bake for about 20 minutes until firm and golden brown. Remove the buns from the oven and turn out on to a rack to cool.
3) Warm the apricot glaze and brush some over each bun. Spread each one with the icing then decorate by cutting small pieces of chocolate matchsticks for eyes and mouths and stick whole matchsticks into the underside of each bun to represent legs.

10
Disco Party
for twenty young teenagers

The Organization

Teenage parties are never easy on the organizer; you will find that once the food is ready and the room set out, you're just not wanted any more! You will also have to contend with varying levels of sophistication and then in the very next minute downright childishness. Is it all worth it? Of course it is!

It is a good idea to make the party as different as possible from the children's parties that up to a year ago your guests may have been attending happily. The disco in itself is very different and by planning to use just one foreign country as a theme for the food you can really ring the changes in that area as well!

Check very carefully before booking your disco. It is most important that they have all the very top records of the moment – light shows and quadrophonic sound are no substitute (especially to teenage girls) for the absence of their favourite groups' singles!

Invitations for this type of party can be great fun if they are written round and round like a record groove on a circular card – definitely a job for the birthday girl (or boy)!

Lots of posters and photos of favourite pop stars (raid the bedrooms!) make colourful and appropriate decorations for the disco area while travel posters and glossy holiday-brochure pages can be used around the tables to great effect, as can flags and coloured ribbons in the chosen country's colours.

Even though there are starters, main courses and sweets, it is best to arrange the food as a buffet, making sure that there are enough places for everyone to sit down – you never know, they may need to rest their feet!

The Food

There are two choices of menu for this party, using either French or Italian food. All the recipes are carefully chosen old favourites – nothing too garlicky or spicy – just excellent examples of the best home cooking from the countries concerned.

THE FRENCH TABLE

Terrine de porc
A coarse farmhouse pâté of pork meat and liver, covered with streaky bacon.

Salade de pommes et crevettes
A delicious and refreshing salad with shrimps or prawns and apples.

Quiche aux oignons
Onion tart, superbly smooth and creamy with a good oniony flavour.

Coq au vin d'Alsace
The white wine version of this classic dish – much lighter than the traditional burgundy-based recipe. (The alcohol evaporates during cooking so it's OK for youngsters to eat!)

Dauphinois potatoes
A really easy way of serving beautifully smooth potatoes.

Baked tomatoes à la Provençal
The simplest of all stuffed tomatoes – very tasty!

Mousse au chocolat
Little pots of rich chocolate mousse are another favourite French concoction.

Tarte Normande
The lovely fresh-tasting apple flan from Normandy. Delicious hot or cold, with cream or ice cream or just as it is!

Cheeses
Serve a selection of French cheeses with biscuits and celery.

THE ITALIAN TABLE

Anti pasto misto
A good hors d'oeuvre of mixed salami, ham, tuna and vegetables.

Bagna cauda
A cream and anchovy sauce, served hot with lots of different vegetables to 'dunk'.

Polpette alla Casalinga
Tender little meatballs served with an aromatic tomato sauce.

Gnocchi di patate
Potato gnocchi – super mixed in the tomato sauce with the meatballs.

Spaghetti alla carbonara
A bacon and egg cheesy sauce, really delicious with thin pasta.

Cassata alla Siciliana
A chilled dessert cake with Ricotta cheese – traditionally served at Easter or at weddings.

Orange granita
A soft water ice, excellent served with wafer biscuits.

Cheeses
Serve a selection of Italian cheeses with biscuits and celery.

The Drinks
Disco dancing is hot work. Have a good selection of fizzy and still drinks at the ready. Lots of ice, orange and lemon slices, straws and cocktail ornaments will all be needed.

If you would like to do a punch type of drink, non-alcoholic Sangria is popular. Chop a good selection of summer fruits into small pieces, cover with grape juice, chill, then add sugar to taste.

Recipes

TERRINE DE PORC

6–8 rashers streaky bacon
400g (1lb) pork
200g (8oz) pig's liver
1 small onion, finely chopped
2 tablespoons port
150g (6oz) fresh brown breadcrumbs
3 eggs
1 teaspoon marjoram
½ teaspoon salt

To make
1) Preheat the oven to 180°C (350°F) Gas Mark 4. Prepare a bain-marie by pouring water into a large roasting tin. Line a loaf tin with the bacon.
2) Mince the pork and liver together. Mix in the onion. Sprinkle the port over the breadcrumbs and leave for a moment or two to soak in.
3) Beat the eggs, then use to bind all the ingredients together. Turn the mixture into the prepared loaf tin and press down.
4) Cover the terrine with foil, then place in the centre of the bain-marie and cook for 1½ hours. Allow to cool. Press overnight using a weight of approx 800g (2lb).

N.B. Pâtés such as this are always best served with crisp French bread and gherkins.

SALADE DE POMMES ET CREVETTES

4 crisp eating apples
200g (8oz) prawns or shrimps, peeled weight
100g (4oz) walnuts, quartered
½ teaspoon lemon juice
¼–½ Webb's lettuce

For the dressing

½ teaspoon French mustard
4 tablespoons single cream
salt and freshly ground black pepper

To make

1) Core and cut the apples into small chunks. Put into a bowl with the prawns and nuts and sprinkle with lemon juice.
2) Wash and dry the lettuce and use to line a large salad bowl or platter.
3) Whisk the mustard into the cream and season well. Pour the dressing over the apples and prawns and turn over gently to coat thoroughly.
4) Pile the apple and prawn salad on top of the lettuce and serve.

QUICHE AUX OIGNONS

For the flan pastry

225g (9oz) flour
salt
150g (6oz) butter, chilled

1 large egg, beaten
2–3 teaspoons cold water

To make

1) Sift the flour and salt into a bowl. Cut the butter into tiny dice and rub into the flour until the mixture resembles fine breadcrumbs.
2) Pour over the egg, add a little water and gather the mixture up into a soft dough. Chill for 30 minutes.
3) Roll out the pastry on a lightly floured board and use to line a 30cm (12in) flan tin. Chill again for 30 minutes. Preheat the oven to 200°C (400°F) Gas Mark 6.
4) Bake the flan for 10–15 minutes. (Pop a piece of screwed-up foil into the flan for the first 7 minutes of cooking time to stop the pastry puffing up in the middle).

For the filling

4 large Spanish onions
50g (2oz) butter
2 large eggs plus 1 egg yolk
450ml (¾pint) double cream
good pinch of nutmeg
¼ teaspoon salt and white pepper

To make

1) Preheat the oven to 190°C (375°F) Gas Mark 5.
2) Peel and slice the onions finely. Melt the butter and cook the onions, covered, until soft but not coloured.
3) Beat the eggs with the cream and seasonings, stir into the onions then turn the whole into the flan case.
4) Bake for 35–40 minutes until golden brown. Serve hot or cold.

N.B. If you feel that all this cream is being wasted on teenagers then substitute half milk, half cream.

COQ AU VIN D'ALSACE

3 tablespoons flour
1 teaspoon salt and freshly ground black pepper
3 roasting chickens, each cut up into 6–8 pieces and
    skinned
100g (4oz) butter
3 bunches spring onions, chopped
450ml (¾pint) Reisling
400g (1lb) mushrooms, wiped and sliced
300ml (½pint) double cream

To make

1) Preheat the oven to 180°C (350°F) Gas Mark 4.
2) Mix the flour with the salt and pepper and roll the chicken pieces in it to coat on all sides.
3) Heat the butter in a large heavy pan and brown the chicken pieces a few at a time. Keep warm.
4) When all the chicken pieces have been browned, add the spring onions to the pan and cook until soft. Return the chicken pieces to the pan, add the wine and mushrooms and cook for 1 hour until the chicken is tender.
5) Remove the chicken pieces and arrange on a serving dish. Cover with foil to keep warm. Boil the cooking juices briskly until reduced by half. Turn the heat to low and slowly add the cream. Stir well, check seasonings and pour the sauce over the chicken pieces. Serve hot.

DAUPHINOIS POTATOES

2kg (5lb) large 'waxy' potatoes
salt and freshly ground black pepper
1 large clove of garlic
100g (4oz) butter
1 litre (1½pints) single cream
enough milk to cover

To make

1) Preheat the oven to 170°C (325°F) Gas Mark 3.
2) Peel and slice the potatoes about 1cm (¼in) thick. Season with salt and pepper.
3) Rub the bases of two large roasting trays with the cut clove of garlic. Spread thickly with butter then arrange the potato slices in layers to a depth of about 4cm (1½in). Pour over the cream and enough milk to cover. Dot the top with any remaining butter.
4) Bake in the oven for 1 hour until golden brown and cooked through.

BAKED TOMATOES À LA PROVENÇAL

10 large tomatoes
200g (8oz) fresh brown breadcrumbs
100g (4oz) freshly chopped parsley
2 cloves garlic, very finely chopped
salt and freshly ground black pepper
2–3 tablespoons olive oil

To make

1) Preheat the oven to 200°C (400°F) Gas Mark 6.
2) Cut the tomatoes in half widthways and scoop out the

flesh and seeds with a small spoon. Turn upside-down to drain.

3) Mix the breadcrumbs, parsley and garlic together and season well. Spoon this mixture into the tomatoes, sprinkle with the oil, set on a baking tray and cook for 15–20 minutes until the crumbs are crisp and golden brown. Serve hot.

MOUSSE AU CHOCOLAT *(enough for 12 small mousse pots or glasses)*

300g (12oz) dark chocolate
4 tablespoons black coffee
25g (1oz) butter
2 drops vanilla essence
6 eggs, separated

To make
1) Melt the chocolate in the coffee with the butter over a very low heat, stirring gently. Add the vanilla essence.
2) Remove the pan from the heat and immediately beat in the egg yolks, one at a time.
3) Whisk the egg whites until very stiff, fold into the chocolate mixture then pour into small pots or glasses and chill well overnight.
4) Serve with cream and small brandy snaps or cigarette russes biscuits.

TARTE NORMANDE

For the flan pastry

150g (6oz) butter
225g (9oz) plain flour

1 teaspoon caster sugar
1 large egg, beaten
2–3 teaspoons cold water

To make

Follow the recipe for flan pastry given for the Quiche aux oignons (on page 149) but cook through completely at 200°C (400°F) Gas Mark 6 for 25–30 minutes.

For the filling

800g (2lb) cooking apples
2 tablespoons water
50g (2oz) sugar (approx)
4 crisp green eating apples
2 tablespoons sugar
150ml (¼pint) water
¼ teaspoon lemon juice
4 tablespoons warmed apricot glaze (see page 00)

To cook

1) Peel and core the cooking apples and cut into chunks. Put into a pan with the 2 tablespoons of water and the 50g (2oz) sugar and cover tightly. Heat very gently and cook until the apples will mash into a smooth purée. Taste for sweetness; they need to be quite sharp.
2) Spread the purée over the bottom of the flan case.
3) Cut the eating apples into quarters and core. Cut each quarter into 2–3 slices.
4) Melt the 2 tablespoons sugar in the 150ml (¼pint) water and add the lemon juice. Add the apple slices and simmer for just 1 minute. Drain well.
5) Arrange the apple slices attractively around the puréed apple. Brush with warm apricot glaze. Serve with whipped cream.

ANTI PASTO MISTO

4 large tomatoes, sliced
freshly ground black pepper
2 fennel bulbs
10 thin slices salami
10 thin slices garlic sausage
10 thin slices mortadella sausage
50g (2oz) black olives
150g (6oz) Mozzarella cheese
4 hard-boiled eggs
2–3 anchovies

To prepare
1) Arrange the tomatoes around the edge of a large salad platter. Season with a little black pepper.
2) Cut the fennel into fours or eights, dependent on size. Arrange on the platter.
3) Arrange the slices of meat round the platter in concentric circles; decorate with the olives.
4) Slice the cheese as thinly as possible; quarter the eggs and garnish with thin strips of anchovy. Arrange the cheese and eggs on the platter. Cover with clingfilm and chill till required.

BAGNA CAUDA

For the sauce

450ml (¾pint) double cream
1 small tin anchovy fillets, drained and soaked in milk for 1 hour
50g (2oz) butter

    1 teaspoon finely chopped garlic
    1 candle warmer and enamel pot

For the 'dippers'

    1 packet of bread sticks
    1 cucumber, seeded and cut into strips 5 × 1cm (2 ×
      ½in)
    4–6 carrots, peeled and cut into strips
    1 head of celery, cut into sticks
    2 green peppers   } seeded and cut into strips
    2 red peppers
    2 bunches of radishes, washed and trimmed

To make

1) Bring the cream to the boil and allow it to simmer for
   about 15 minutes until it has reduced to about 300ml
   (½pint) and has thickened.
2) Drain the anchovies and chop finely. Melt the butter in
   the enamel pot but do not allow to brown. Add the
   anchovies and garlic then finally the reduced cream.
3) Heat the mixture but do not allow to boil. Serve (using
   the candle warmer to keep the sauce hot) surrounded
   by the bread sticks and vegetables for 'dipping'.
   (Should the sauce separate – beat back together with a
   whisk.)

There is another sauce for this dish based on oil rather
than cream – not quite so elegant but still good.

    150ml (¼pint) olive oil
    75g (3oz) butter
    2 cloves garlic, chopped finely
    2 tins anchovies, drained and chopped

To make

1) Heat the oil and butter together, add the garlic and cook gently for 2 minutes.
2) Add the anchovies and simmer over a very low heat for 10 minutes. Serve as above.

POLPETTE ALLA CASALINGA

800g (2lb) chuck steak
200g (8oz) pork
4 slices white bread, cut into small pieces
4 tablespoons milk
2 eggs, beaten
2 tablespoons freshly chopped parsley
2 teaspoons olive oil
½ teaspoon finely chopped garlic
1 teaspoon salt and some freshly ground black pepper

olive oil for frying

To make

1) Trim the meats of all fat then mince finely, twice.
2) Soak the bread in the milk then thoroughly mix all the ingredients together, adding a little more oil if the mixture appears too dry. Beat well until smooth.
3) Dampen your hands and form small meatballs about 3cm (1¼in) in diameter. Chill for 1 hour.
4) Heat the oil in a large heavy pan. Fry the meatballs over a moderate heat, shaking the pan to keep their shape. The cooking will probably need to be done in 2–3 batches. Keep the cooked meatballs hot. Serve with tomato sauce.

TOMATO SAUCE

3 tablespoons olive oil
150g (6oz) onions, finely chopped
800g (2lb) tinned Italian plum tomatoes, chopped but
    not drained
2 tablespoons tomato purée
1 teaspoon basil
¼ teaspoon thyme
1 teaspoon sugar
1 teaspoon salt
freshly ground black pepper

To make
1) Heat the oil in a large heavy pan and cook the onions
   until they are soft and light brown.
2) Add the tomatoes, tomato purée, herbs, sugar, salt and
   pepper. Reduce the heat and simmer for 40 minutes.
3) Press through a fine sieve; check the seasonings. Serve
   hot.

GNOCCHI DI PATATE

1.2kg (3lb) potatoes, peeled
450g (1lb 2oz) flour
3 eggs, beaten
salt
good pinch of nutmeg
100g (4oz) butter
50g (2oz) Parmesan cheese, grated

To make
1) Boil the potatoes in salted water until cooked. Drain
   well.

2) Mash the potatoes then add the flour, eggs, salt and nutmeg and mix together well.

3) Lightly flour a board; turn the potato mixture on to it and roll into long sausage shapes 2cm (¾in) thick. Cut into 2.5cm (1in) lengths and make a dent in the middle of each gnocchi.

4) Bring a large pan of salted water to the boil and drop in the gnocchi a few at a time. Cook for a few minutes, until they rise to the surface. Preheat the grill.

5) Butter two large round ovenproof dishes. When each batch of gnocchi is cooked put them into the dishes in a circular, overlapping pattern. Keep hot in a warm oven.

6) To finish, dot with the remaining butter, sprinkle with cheese and grill until well browned. Serve at once.

SPAGHETTI ALLA CARBONARA

2kg (5lb) spaghetti
salt
3 tablespoons olive oil
2 large onions, thinly sliced
2 cloves garlic, finely chopped
400g (1lb) bacon, derinded and cut into 1cm (½in) strips
4 eggs
150g (3oz) Parmesan cheese, grated
150ml (¼pint) single cream
salt and freshly ground black pepper
2 tablespoons freshly chopped parsley

To make

1) Bring a large pan of lightly salted water to the boil and cook the spaghetti for 10 minutes. Drain well.

2) Meanwhile, heat the oil in a frying pan, add the onions and cook until soft but not brown. Add the garlic and cook for a further minute.
3) Add the bacon, turn up the heat and cook for a further 2–3 minutes.
4) In a bowl, beat together the eggs, cheese, cream and parsley. Season well.
5) Mix the drained spaghetti with the bacon, pour over the egg mixture, mix thoroughly and serve at once.

N.B. Normally the heat from the spaghetti is enough to cook the eggs, but when using larger quantities it is better to do the final mixing over a low heat.

CASSATA ALLA SICILIANA

For the cake

> 3 eggs
> 75g (3oz) caster sugar
> ½ teaspoon lemon juice
> ½ teaspoon vanilla essence
> 75g (3oz) plain flour

To make
1) Preheat the oven to 190°C (375°F) Gas Mark 5. Line and grease a 23cm (9in) loaf tin.
2) Beat the eggs and sugar together in a bowl placed over a pan of hot water. When the mixture is pale and so thick that the beaters leave a trail when lifted, beat in the lemon and vanilla.
3) Sift in the flour and fold into the mixture with a metal spoon. Turn into the loaf tin and bake for 25 minutes, or until firm. Cool on a wire rack.

For the filling and covering

400g (1lb) Ricotta cheese
100g (4oz) caster sugar
2 tablespoons Cointreau
50g (2oz) dark chocolate, chopped finely
6 glacé cherries, chopped finely
50g (2oz) chopped mixed peel
1 tablespoon chopped almonds
2 tablespoons orange juice

To make

1) Beat the cheese with the sugar until very smooth; add the liqueur.
2) Divide the mixture into two portions and add the chocolate, cherries, peel and nuts to one half.
3) Cut the cake into three lengthways. Sprinkle each section with the orange juice then sandwich together with the chunky filling.
4) Spread the outside of the cake with the smooth filling and decorate with cherries, grated chocolate or anything else you have available.

ORANGE GRANITA

450ml (¾pint) water
150g (6oz) sugar
450ml (¾pint) orange juice
juice of 1 lemon

To make

1) Bring the water and sugar to the boil over a medium heat. Stir to dissolve the sugar.

2) When the syrup boils, time it for exactly 5 minutes. Let it cool. Stir in the fruit juices.

3) Freeze in open trays, scraping the ice crystals into the middle every 30 minutes or so.

4) The finished water–ice should have a very light texture almost like snow. Serve with really super wafer biscuits.

11
Bonfire Party
for children of all ages

The Organization

Safety has to be the most important item to consider when planning a bonfire party. Choosing where to site the bonfire and where to let off the fireworks will need some careful thought. Have a get-together with all the helpers well before the event to plan exactly who does what and to work out budgets to cover the cost of fireworks and food.

You will need to decide whether the food is to be eaten indoors or outside, so that provision can be made for placing large dustbins in strategic positions for the easy disposal of used plates and cartons. It will be far easier if paper 'crockery' is used but it needs to be of the stronger type that withstands hot food. The only cutlery needed

will be forks – and you will definitely need a lot of paper napkins.

Standing round a good bonfire, well wrapped against the cold, munching toffee apples while watching the firelight flickering on happy faces, is a strong childhood memory for most adults. Careful planning and watchful supervision on the night will ensure that your young guests' memories are very special too!

The Food

The quantities given in the recipes will serve 25 people.

Lamb hot-pot
Cooking facilities may be limited so it's best to choose a one-pot meal. The lamb is cubed as are the vegetables so the hot-pot is easily eaten with a fork. It can be made the day before and then re-heated; in fact it taste better after a day's rest.

Spicy tomato soup
A warming broth for a cold night always tastes better when drunk in the open air.

Toffee apples
Easy to make and usually much better than the bought variety. Start saving lolly sticks in the early spring!

Bonfire toffee
A really lovely chewy treacle toffee. Part of its charm is in the funny-shaped pieces obtained by bashing with a hammer to break it into more sensible sizes.

Parkin
A traditional oatmeal and ginger cake, it is a little sticky and so moist it doesn't need buttering at all.

N.B. All the food suggested for this children's party would be quite suitable for grown-ups too; just adjust one or two of the seasonings slightly.

The Drinks

Warm comforting drinks will be needed for this party and although many children will probably just have the soup, an alternative savoury drink such as Bovril would be a good idea. Hot whisked drinking chocolate or Horlicks are also popular provided you have a place where you can boil the milk quickly.

Recipes

LAMB HOT-POT

3 large shoulders of lamb weighing about 2kg (4½lb)
  each
100g (4oz) plain flour
2 tablespoons mixed herbs
50g (2oz) butter
2 tablespoons vegetable oil
3 large onions, peeled and sliced
1 head of celery, chopped
600g (1½lb) carrots, chopped
2.5kg (5lb) potatoes
salt and freshly ground black pepper
1.8 litres (3pints) meat stock, hot

To make

1) Preheat the oven to 180°C (350°F) Gas Mark 4.
2) Bone out the meat, trim away the fat and any gristle,
   then cut into 3cm (1¼in) cubes. Mix together the flour
   and herbs and toss the meat cubes in the mixture.
3) Melt the butter in the oil and brown the meat a few
   pieces at a time. Put into deep casserole dishes.
4) When all the meat has been browned, fry the onions
   and celery until soft and light brown and add to the
   meat. Mix in the carrots.
5) Peel and cube the potatoes, add to the meat and
   vegetables and season well. Pour over the hot stock.
   Cook slowly in the oven for 2–2½ hours, until the
   meat is very tender.

6) If you have cooked the meat one day earlier, before re-heating skim off any fat that may have solidified on the top.

SPICY TOMATO SOUP

100g (4oz) butter
4 tablespoons oil
4.5kg (10–12lb) ripe tomatoes, cut up
4 large onions, thinly sliced
4.5 litres (10–12pints) chicken stock
1 tablespoon dried thyme
1 teaspoon cayenne pepper
salt
2–4 tablespoons Worcestershire sauce (optional)

To make
1) Heat the butter and oil in a large pan, cook the tomatoes and onions until very soft.
2) Push the vegetables through a sieve into another large pan. Add the stock and seasonings, simmer for 20 minutes.
3) Check for salt and serve with a dash of Worcestershire sauce, if liked.

TOFFEE APPLES

25 medium-sized eating apples
25 lolly sticks
1.2kg (3lb) demerara sugar
150g (6oz) butter
2 tablespoons vinegar

450ml (¾pint) water
3 tablespoons golden syrup

you will also need a sugar thermometer

To make

Unless you have a preserving pan it will be easier to make the apples in two or three batches following the method through.

1) Wipe the apples and push in the lolly sticks.
2) Using a heavy-based pan, put in the remaining ingredients and heat until the sugar melts.
3) Boil steadily until the temperature reaches 143°C (290°F) on a sugar thermometer.
4) Remove the pan from the heat and dip in each apple one by one, spinning the apple slowly in the toffee to coat it well.
5) Put the apples on to silicone paper or a well-buttered baking sheet and leave to set.

BONFIRE TOFFEE

900g (2¼lb) demerara sugar
6 tablespoons golden syrup
3 tablespoons black treacle
300g (12oz) butter
300ml (½pint) water

you will also need a sugar thermometer

To make
1) Butter 3 tins measuring 15cm (6in) square.
2) Put all the ingredients into a large heavy-based pan and

stir over a low heat until the butter melts and the sugar dissolves.

3) Bring to the boil and cover the pan; boil gently for 2 minutes.

4) Take off the lid and continue boiling very gently until a temperature of 149°C (300°F) is reached on a sugar thermometer. This should take some 10–15 minutes. Pour the mixture into the buttered tins and allow to set.

5) When the toffee is hard, turn it out on to a board and break it into small pieces with a hammer.

PARKIN

600g (1½lb) plain flour
1½ teaspoons salt
25g (1oz) bicarbonate of soda
3 teaspoons mixed spice
500g (1¼lb) soft brown sugar
300g (12oz) coarse oatmeal
300g (12oz) butter
400g (1lb) golden syrup
450ml (¾pint) milk

To make

1) Preheat the oven to 180°C (350°F) Gas Mark 4. Grease 2 large roasting tins.

2) Sift the flour, salt, bicarbonate of soda together. Mix in the sugar, oatmeal and spice.

3) Melt the butter in the syrup over a low heat, whisk in the milk, pour on to the flour mixture and beat well.

4) Pour into the prepared tins and bake for 50–60 minutes.

N.B. This parkin can be made in advance and kept, well wrapped in foil, for 2–3 days before use.

12
Party Games

One of the most surprising things learnt from our questionaires was that today's children play and enjoy exactly the same games at parties as their parents and grandparents did.

There are several really comprehensive books of games on the market if you need help, but according to the kids interviewed, the best games are:

TREASURE HUNTS

This can range from a simple 'find the thimble' to a complex series of clues for older children. Treasure hunts are easily organized and are one of the best ways of keeping early arrivals occupied while you welcome other guests.

Preparation
Gather together the items to be 'hunted' and hide them around the room bearing in mind the age and height of the 'searchers'. Don't put the items behind a 'breakable' or anything you would prefer not to have turned upside down! If the children are older you need not hunt for treasure as such, but give each one a series of clues to solve – nothing too difficult, try to amuse rather than perplex.

To play
Show your guests exactly what it is they are to find. Point younger children directly towards their first 'find'. That

way you can ensure that everyone has at least one 'treasure' at the end of the game.

CAT AND MOUSE

A terrible game – the mice squeal and scream 'blue murder', then cry when caught by the cat. Our panel insisted they enjoy it!

Preparation
You will need a scarf to use as a blindfold for the cat.

To play
Once it has been decided who is to be the 'cat', the 'mice' then form a circle around him or her and put their hands in the air. The cat is blindfolded then is spun round three times. The mice disperse and the cat runs after them. As he or she catches each mouse they form a chain holding on to the cat until all are caught. The first 'mouse' to be caught then becomes the 'cat'.

BLIND MAN'S BUFF

Make sure there's a reasonable amount of space when playing this game. It's amazing how many items a pair of flailing arms can hit!

Preparation
You will need a scarf to use as a blindfold.

To play
First choose one guest to be 'on'. Tie the scarf around their eyes and twirl them round three times. All the other

players take up positions after the blindfold goes on but they must not move their feet once the game starts, although crouching, bending or swaying movements are allowed. When the blindfolded player finds another player that child is then 'on'!

PIN THE TAIL ON THE DONKEY

Easy to adapt to fit in with any party's theme. A good sitting-down game (and you do need some).

Preparation
You will need a scarf, a piece of pinboard, a good picture of a donkey and a tail (made by plaiting a few scraps of wool) stuck through the top end with a pin.

To play
Each child takes turns at putting on the blindfold then trying to pin the tail on to the donkey in the correct place; the child nearest to the right position is the winner.

MUSICAL CHAIRS, HATS, BUMPS AND STATUES

Any game played to music seems very popular. If you haven't room for the chairs play bumps or statues.

Preparation
For musical chairs you need to place dining chairs alternately facing in opposite directions in a long line, or in a circle facing outwards. Either way you will need one less chair then the number of children playing.

For musical hats you will need one less hat than the numbers playing.

To play

Chairs: start the music and make the children walk around the chairs; when the music stops they must sit down on a chair. The child left standing is out. Another chair is removed and the music re-started; carry on until just one child is left as the winner.

Hats: start the music and make the children sit down and pass the hats from head to head; when the music stops whoever hasn't got a hat on is out. Continue until just one child is left as the winner.

Bumps: start the music and make the children dance about; when the music stops they must 'bump' down on the floor. Last one down is out. Continue until only one child is left as the winner.

Statues: start the music and make the children run or dance about until it stops when they must stay completely still – if they move they are out. Continue until just one child is left as the winner.

DEAD LIONS

A really funny game, absolutely hilarious to watch.

Preparation

Choose someone to be 'on'.

To play

Everyone else lies down on the floor. The child who is 'on' must then make the dead lions roar with laughter.

Any methods are allowed except touching. As each lion 'roars' they are out, the last one to be out is the next 'on'.

WHO AM I?

Preparation
Write some names on large pieces of paper. They can be of famous people or drawn from the children in the room. You will need a safety pin to secure each piece of paper.

To play
Pin a name to the back of each child; they must try to find out who they are by asking questions of the other children.

CHINESE WHISPERS

To play
Sit everyone down in a circle. A message is whispered from child to child; comparing the first and last message can be very funny.

PASS THE PARCEL

Even the three-year-olds mentioned this game as a favourite!

Preparation
Wrap a small present in layer after layer of paper.

To play
Sit everyone in a circle. When the music starts the children pass the parcel from one to another. When the music

stops the child holding the parcel removes one layer of paper. Repeat until the last layer is reached; the present goes to the child who removes the final layer.

MURDER

Preparation
Allow one piece of paper per guest. On one piece write 'detective', on another write 'murderer', and leave the remaining pieces blank. Put the papers into a hat and let your guests take one each. The 'murderer' must not declare his identity.

To play
Send the 'detective' out of the room and turn off the light. The 'murderer' touches the person of his or her choice who then lies down as dead. When the light is switched on the 'detective' returns and solves the crime by asking questions. Everyone *must* tell the truth with the exception of the murderer.

SPIN THE BOTTLE

Preparation
Have a list of forfeits ready – put a funny hat on and sing a song, kiss the best-looking boy in the room, etc. You will also need an empty glass bottle and some little prizes.

To play
Sit everyone down in a circle; the bottle is placed on its side and each child takes a turn at spinning it. When it stops whoever it points towards has to do a forfeit or receives a small prize.

Index

Cookery handbooks now available in Panther Books

L D Michaels
The Complete Book of Pressure Cooking   £1.95 ☐

Cecilia Norman
Pancakes & Pizzas   95p ☐
Microwave Cookery Course   £1.95 ☐
The Pie and Pastry Cookbook   £2.50 ☐
Barbecue Cookery   £1.50 ☐

Franny Singer
The Slow Crock Cookbook   £1.95 ☐

Janet Walker
Vegetarian Cookery   £1.50 ☐

Pamela Westland
Bean Feast   £1.95 ☐
The Complete Grill Cookbook   £1.50 ☐
High-Fibre Vegetarian Cookery   £1.95 ☐

Marika Hanbury Tenison
Deep-Freeze Cookery   £1.95 ☐
Cooking with Vegetables   £1.95 ☐

Sheila Howarth
Grow, Freeze and Cook   £1.50 ☐

Jennifer Stone
The Alcoholic Cookbook   £1.25 ☐

Beryl Wood
Let's Preserve It   £1.50 ☐

Barbara Griggs
Baby's Cookbook   £1.95 ☐

Wendy Craig
Busy Mum's Cookbook   £1.95 ☐

Carolyn Heal and Michael Allsop
Cooking with Spices   £2.95 ☐

To order direct from the publisher just tick the titles you want
and fill in the order form.

All these books are available at your local bookshop or newsagent, or can be ordered direct from the publisher.,

To order direct from the publisher just tick the titles you want and fill in the form below.

Name _____

Address _____

_____

Send to:
Panther Cash Sales
PO Box 11, Falmouth, Cornwall TR10 9EN.

Please enclose remittance to the value of the cover price plus:

UK 45p for the first book, 20p for the second book plus 14p per copy for each additional book ordered to a maximum charge of £1.63.

BFPO and Eire 45p for the first book, 20p for the second book plus 14p per copy for the next 7 books, thereafter 8p per book.

Overseas 75p for the first book and 21p for each additional book.

_____

Panther Books reserve the right to show new retail prices on covers, which may differ from those previously advertised in the text or elsewhere.